695

Folktales of French Canada

Also by Edith Fowke
Folk Songs of Canada, 1954
Chansons de Québec/Folk Songs of Quebec, 1957
Canada's Story in Song, 1960
Traditional Singers and Songs from Ontario, 1965
Songs of Work and Freedom, 1965
Folk Songs of Canada II, 1967
Sally Go Round the Sun, 1969
Lumbering Songs from the Northern Woods, 1970
The Penguin Book of Canadian Folk Songs, 1973
Folklore of Canada, 1976
Ring Around the Moon, 1977

(Editor, Logging with Paul Bunyan by John D. Robbins, 1967)
(Notes, Canadian Vibrations canadiennes, 1972)

Folktales
of
French Canada

Edith Fowke

NC PRESS LIMITED
TORONTO, 1979

Cover illustration "la chasse-galerie" by Henri Julien.
Section illustrations by Henri Julien.

Canadian Cataloguing in Publication Data
Main entry under title:

Folktales of French Canada

Bibliography: p.
Includes index.
ISBN 0-919601-01-4

1. Tales, Canadian (French)* I. Fowke, Edith Fulton, 1913-

GR113.F65   398.2'09714   C79-094599-1

We would like to thank the Ontario Arts Council and the Canada Council
for their assitance in the production of this book.

New Canada Publications, a division of NC Press Limited, Box 4010, Sta-
tion A, Toronto, Ontario, M5W 1H8. (416) 368-1165.

Contents

Foreword

French Canadians have preserved by far the largest and most interesting heritage of folktales in this country, but most of them are unknown to Anglo-Canadians. This small collection has two main aims: to present a number of French-Canadian tales in translations that follow the originals as closely as possible, and to give examples of the various kinds of tales that fall within the scope of oral literature.

Some previously published books present French-Canadian tales in English, but in nearly all of these the authors have retold the tales in their own words, preserving the plots but not the style or the phrasing of the originals. The tales in this book differ from them in that they are direct translations, not adaptations or re-creations. The object is to give English versions that adhere as closely as possible to the way the original narrators told the stories. Of course any translation can only approximate the style of the original.

Because the French-Canadian repertoire is so large and so varied, it is possible to choose from it examples of the many different kinds of tales that have circulated orally through the ages. The two main classes are the legends, or stories that are believed by the people who tell them, and the more general folktales that are told as fiction.

Stith Thompson, the major authority on the folktale, has subdivided the fictional tales into four groups: "Animal Tales," "Ordinary Folktales" (which include the *Märchen* or fairy tales, and romantic tales), the shorter and simpler "Jokes and Anecdotes," and the smaller group of "Formula Tales." The stories chosen illustrate all of these varieties, as well as the legends. This selection should therefore be useful to those interested in studying folktales in general, as well as to those interested in this particular form of French-Canadian literature.

Luc Lacourcière, the pre-eminent authority on French-Canadian folklore, has explained why his people's heritage of folktales is so rich. In a 1961 survey of "The Present State of French-Canadian Folklore Studies" he wrote:

> From the beginning of Canadian history to the middle of the nineteenth century folklore and oral tradition were in

what we could call un âge d'or. They continued develop-
ing naturally and spontaneously. Even the Seven Years'
War and the cession of Canada to the English offered no
obstacles; quite the contrary, these important historical
events created a new climate in which the peasant's at-
tachment to the soil became more pronounced and his
French traditions more deeply rooted. Because of the atti-
tude of the king of France who never allowed the estab-
lishment of a press in New France, and the English govern-
ment which consistently after the conquest of Canada used
English as an instrument of propaganda for introducing
that language and Protestantism, there was a complete lack
of publication in French and a scarcity of French schools.
This period, which appears to some historians as a new
dark age, was truly the golden age of oral literature.

Dr. Marius Barbeau began to harvest that oral literature in
1914. Between then and 1935 he gathered tales and songs in
Beauce, Kamouraska, Charlevoix, Saguenay, and the Gaspé
peninsula, and he also recruited other collectors such as E.-Z.
Massicotte, Evelyn Bolduc, Gustave Lanctôt, and Adélard Lambert. Extensive sections of their collections appeared in the
Journal of American Folklore between 1916 and 1950 when
Barbeau was an associate editor. Since then folktale collecting
has continued apace, especially under Luc Lacourcière at l'U-
niversité Laval, and Father Germain Lemieux at l'Université de
Sudbury. However, the selections for this book have been
drawn largely from the tales published in the *Journal of American Folklore*. As these were the earliest tales collected I felt
that they would represent most closely "the golden age of oral
literature" of which Lacourcière wrote.

Most of the tales selected were presented by the collector as
he had them directly from a folk narrator. That is the most authentic form of folklore. Almost as valuable are those that
came from Adélard Lambert who had heard them in his youth
from his mother and other members of his family. Later, when
grown up, he wrote the stories out and gave them to Dr. Barbeau. These are somewhat different from the tales noted directly from the lips of storytellers, for M. Lambert was recon-
structing the tales many years after he had heard them.

Consequently, as Gustave Lanctôt points out, they do not reproduce the flavour of the local speech in which they were originally told. However, they came from Lambert's own family, and although he may not remember the exact words in which he heard them, his stories are obviously part of a vital folklore tradition.

A little farther removed from tradition are the two legends, "The Devil at the Dance" and "The Devil Builds a Church," which Dr. J.-E.-A. Cloutier communicated to Dr. Barbeau in 1919. He had heard them from people at L'Islet some thirty years earlier. Both of these are detailed and localized versions of legends that have been reported from many other localities in Quebec. Dr. Cloutier wrote that he had retold the legends as exactly as his memory allowed after such a long space of time, believing that he ought to reproduce the original language of the storyteller with the greatest fidelity possible.

However, it should be noted that they lack the direct speech of the original storytellers because they were filtered through Dr. Cloutier's memory, and they are somewhat further removed from folk tradition than those from Adélard Lambert: he was telling stories that had come to him in the traditional manner through his own family, while Dr. Cloutier was more of an outsider in the community where he heard the tales. As Dr. Barbeau wrote in introducing the Cloutier items: "Although the language is quite characteristic of the Canadian land in general, it is not strictly that of a particular district. Probably influenced by the well-known style of the writer Louis Fréchette, Dr. Cloutier has outdone the original text with the object of making it more entertaining." Thus his stories are a step removed from the most authentic form of the folktales, but there is no doubt that they are folk rather than literary versions: even though the language is not directly transcribed, the plot details parallel other versions coming directly from the folk, and he does mention his sources.

Two other legends are still further removed from the folk. These are Honoré Beaugrand's version of "The Chasse Galerie" and Joseph-Charles Taché's version of "Cadieux's Lament." The tales themselves are two of the best known and most widespread of all French-Canadian legends, but these versions are reported by literary men who have undoubtedly heard the oral tales but who present them in their own style.

I have chosen to use their versions for several reasons: they are among the earliest reports of the legends; they are the most detailed; and they are good examples of how nineteenth-century literary figures interpreted French-Canadian folklore. The most famous example of such interpretation is Philippe Aubert de Gaspé's version of "Rose Latulippe," but that is more definitely fictionalized, containing details not found in oral versions. Beaugrand and Taché embroidered the oral legends stylistically, but they did not add fictional plot elements. Indeed, both emphasize that they had heard the legends from voyageurs and lumberjacks, and both present them in the form of oral narratives: Taché attributes his to an old guide, Morache, while Beaugrand puts his in the mouth of a lumbercamp cook. Both are good imitations of the traditional story-telling style, but careful readers will note colourful touches that owe more to literary pens than to the tongues of unlettered voyageurs. Comparing these two versions with other more authentic tales will give the reader some insight into the differences between genuine oral narratives and literary re-creations of folktales.

The fictional tales are arranged in groups according to Stith Thompson's classification, with the section on legends following. Introductions to each section give brief comments on the group as a whole and on the individual tales. The end-matter includes some information on the informants, sources and references for each tale, indexes of the tale types and motifs, and a fairly extensive bibliography of French-Canadian folktales. I hope that this arrangement will make the book useful both for general readers and for folklorists.

Edith Fowke

I Animal Tales

Animal tales form the first of the four groups into which fictional folktales are divided. These were much commoner in earlier times: fables and other stories in which animals took on human characteristics formed a large part of the traditional tales of the Middle Ages. In more recent times cartoons of Mickey Mouse and Donald Duck, tales of Brer Rabbit, and a recent literary best-seller, Watership Down, continue to exploit this type of story.

"The Bear and the Fox" is a very old and famous animal tale found in many countries. For a thousand years a whole cycle of tales in which the sly fox outwits a stupid bear or wolf circulated orally in northern Europe and from there spread to the rest of Europe, to Africa, and to North America, with the protagonists changing with the locale.

These tales also formed part of the famous literary epic usually referred to as the Reynard cycle. Stith Thompson notes that "the tale of how the fox played godfather appears in the Reynard cycle though its origin seems to be in the northern Germanic countries," and that "of all the stories belonging to this general cycle, this is perhaps best known in other parts of the world than central Europe. It is to be found in most parts of Asia, all over Africa, in the Negro, the Spanish, the Portuguese, and the French traditions in America, and among the North American Indians." The French-Canadian version that follows is a particularly fine example: the details of the crying fox and the consoling bear add lively personality touches to what is often a rather commonplace narrative.

"Give Me Back My Purse" is a quite different type: it is an interesting offshoot of some well-known stories that are classified as animal tales although they deal partly or wholly with objects. Stith Thompson describes one type that somewhat resembles the French-Canadian version: "Aarne conceives that the original Asiatic form tells how an egg, a scorpion, a needle, a piece of dung and a mortar (or some other hard object) go together on a journey. They find themselves in the house of an old woman during her absence and hide themselves in various places, lying in wait to harm her. Each attacks her in his characteristic fashion and drive her forth or kill her. This form of the tale is found in India, Indonesia, Malaysia, China, and Japan, and it has spread over a good part of Europe. The corresponding tale in Europe, however, has as its actors a group of animals who hide themselves in a wolf's den or a robber's home. The hiding and the attack on the returning owner are the same in all forms of the tale." The bisected cock with its three unusual allies seems to be peculiar to Quebec, but its relationship to the older tales is obvious.

1   The Fable of The Bear and The Fox

Once upon a time, I'd like to tell you, there was a fox and a
bear. One fine morning during the winter the little fox goes into
a snowbank in front of the bear's house and starts to howl,
howl. Coming out of his house, the bear asks, "What are you
howling about, little fox?"

He replies, "They've sent for me to be godfather, but I don't
want to go."

"My little fox, go then, they're going to give you fine food to
eat. If they sent for me like that I'd gladly go, me who can only
lick my paw."

The little fox starts out, turns around, enters the bear's pantry without being seen, and begins to eat the contents of the
butter tub. When the bear sees him passing again he asks,
"What did you call him, your godson?"

"Oh," he says, "I called him Begun."

The next morning the little fox comes back again to the
snowbank in front of the bear's and he howls, howls.

"What is it, my little fox, that makes you howl so much?"

"Don't talk to me. They've sent for me again to be godfather,
but me, I don't want to go."

"Go on then. They look after you well when you're godfather."

Then the little fox starts out, turns around, enters the bear's
pantry without being seen, and eats half the butter in the tub.
Seeing him passing again, the bear asks him, "What did you
call him, your godson?"

"I called him Half Done."

"That's a fine name, my little fox. It isn't right to pester you
like that to be godfather."

Again the same thing—the next morning, the little fox plants
himself in the snowbank and starts to howl. Howl, howl, my
little fox. The bear asks, "But why howl so much, my little
fox?"

"They've asked me again to be godfather, and me, I don't
want to go."

"My little fox, go on then. You always return well fed when

you are godfather. If someone would invite me I'd ask nothing better."

Turning around, the little fox enters the bear's pantry where he eats the rest of the butter in the tub. Seeing him pass again, the bear asks, "What did you call him, your godson?"

"I called him Bottom-Licked."

The bear replies, "That's a fine name, that, my little fox. I'd like them to call me to be godfather, me who can only lick my paw."

When he goes to look for some butter in his tub, the bear finds all the butter gone. Going to see the fox, he says, "My little fox, I think you've played a trick on me. You said that they called you to be godfather, but it's all lies. You went to eat my tub of butter. The names you said were Begun, Half Done, and Bottom-Licked, but, my little fox, I'll eat you right now."

"Don't eat me this instant when you're angry. Look, we're both going to bed and the one who tomorrow morning will have butter on his backside, that will be the one who has eaten the butter." The bear finally agrees and they lie down and sleep.

During the night the fox gets up and puts some butter on the bear's backside. Realizing that he is greased when he wakes, the bear says, "Then it was me who ate it."

Down the road a little farther on the little fox says, "I've played a trick on the bear. You're not very smart, I guarantee, so go lick your paw right now."

And me, they sent me here to tell you that the little fox is indeed smarter than the bear.

2 Give Me Back My Purse!

Once upon a time there was an old man and an old woman who were very poor, so poor that they often spent whole days without having a bit of bread to put in their mouths. If, as the old man quoted the common saying, poverty is no vice, it was at least for them a source of never-ending quarrels.

One day the only cock the old couple owned uncovered a purse filled with silver when scratching the ground. That should have brought happiness and peace to the household, but instead what happened was that the old woman grew very angry with her husband. You see, when the old woman saw the purse she ran to pick it up and hide it carefully so that her husband wouldn't know about it, but she counted without the cock. It followed her and, perching on the window, sang without stopping the disagreeable refrain: "Give me back my purse! Give me back my purse! Give me back my purse!"

That evening when the husband came home he was surprised to hear the cock and asked his wife what it was talking about. The old woman put him off, saying that the cock was crazy, and as disagreeable as he was, and that the sooner they both went away the sooner she'd be rid of them. One word led to another, the quarrel became heated, and the husband decided to go away and take the cock with him, but the old woman wouldn't hear of that.

Shaking with rage, she said to her husband that when he went it wasn't fair for him to take all that they had, and that the cock should be divided into two equal parts. At last, yielding to his wife's protests, the husband agreed to the division and they cut the cock in two, the old woman keeping the back half. The old man took the front half, but he couldn't bring himself to cook and eat it. So he made a back for the cock out of a piece of cloth which he stuffed with straw and went off carrying his cock under his arm.

He walked for two or three weeks, wandering from village to village, begging for his food. As it was fall and getting cold, and the roads were bad, he was very despondent and decided to go back home and endure his wife's abuse rather than continue this roving and miserable life.

As he went back, still carrying his cock under his arm, he

saw a swarm of bees who said to the cock, "My good cock, winter is coming and it's very cold. Will you take us with you?" "Very well," said the cock. "Crawl into my straw back and you'll be quite warm." The bees did as they were told, and the man went on his way.

When he was in the middle of a wood he had to cross, he met a wolf who said to the cock, "Good cock, soon winter is coming and it's going to be cold; will you take me with you?" "Yes," said the cock. "Climb into my straw back."

When they came to the other side of the wood the old man saw a spring which said to the cock, "Good cock, winter is coming; the cold as usual will freeze my water; will you take me with you?" "Yes," said the cock. "Climb into my straw back."

On reaching home, the old man put the cock in the barn and returned to the house. He found his wife at the table having a good meal. More than a little surprised to find his wife in a good humour which led her to invite him to eat with her, the old man ate hungrily for he had walked all that day without eating. When bedtime came, harmony seemed to reign between the couple.

But next morning discord returned to the household. When they woke what was the surprise and the anger of the old woman to hear the cock, which had come to perch on the window, sing loudly: "Give me back my purse! Give me back my purse! Give me back my purse!"

"What, you old fool, you dare to bring that crazy cock! Get up right away and put it in the sheep pen. The two sheep I bought yesterday will soon make a mouthful of that straw back you put on him."

The old man sadly took his cock to the sheep pen. He had promised to obey his wife to keep the peace and he had to live with the consequences.

When the cock was thrown into the sheep pen he asked the wolf to help him and said, "If you want to spend the winter warmly with me it's time to come to my aid and get rid of these sheep." The cock didn't need to repeat the invitation. The wolf asked nothing better than to jump on the sheep. He killed them both in a flash. Rid of the sheep, the cock went back to perch on the window and started singing, "Give me back my purse! Give me back my purse! Give me back my purse!"

"Look here, old man," said his wife, "You didn't put the cock in the sheep pen." "Yes I did." The old woman went to see and found her two sheep dead. "Old man, your cock has killed my sheep. As I've lit the fire to bake some bread you're going to throw the cock into the oven and roast him. That way we'll be rid of him."

The old man took the cock and threw him into the oven, but the cock asked the spring to help him, saying, "If you don't put out this fire you won't be able to spend the winter warmly with me." The spring asked nothing better than to put out the fire and the cock returned to the window and sang, "Give me back my purse! Give me back my purse! Give me back my purse!"

"Look here, old man," said his wife in a rage, "You didn't put the cock in the oven as I told you." "Yes, I did." The old woman went to see and found her fire out. Filled with anger, she caught the cock and said, "I'll see to it myself this time. I'm going to wring this crazy cock's neck."

She took the cock between her knees and began to twist its neck. But the cock said, "Bees, bees, help me or you won't be able to spend the winter warmly in my straw back." At this the bees came out and started to sting the old woman until she yelled and complained, and at last she said, "Call off your bees, cock, and I'll give you your purse."

The cock stopped the bees, the old woman went to look for the purse which she gave to the cock, and the cock gave the purse to his master in return for the straw back he'd made for him. When the master had the purse to live on, everything went well and peace reigned in the household. And the cock lived on for many years in spite of his straw back.

II Ordinary Folktales

The largest group of French-Canadian folktales are the "contes populaires" which correspond to the German Märchen and the English fairy tales. They can be subdivided into tales that involve the supernatural: "contes merveilleux" or "Tales of Magic," and "contes pseudo-merveilleux" or "Romantic Tales" in which the outcome depends more on cleverness and skill than on magic. Most of these show little religious influence although a few deal with religious themes. Many of them are thought to have their roots in a pre-Christian era, and most of their plots are widespread in Europe and Asia. They illustrate the characteristics of the typical folktale: repetition by threes, emphasis on trials and quests, the triumph of the youngest son, magic objects and supernatural helpers, marvelous transformations, and happy endings.

Transformations play a large part in both legends and folktales in French-Canada. The Devil can be transformed into a handsome gentleman, a horse, or a black dog; and a sinful man may be transformed into a loup-garou or a feu-follet, and many persons firmly believe in such metamorphoses.

The transformations in ordinary folktales usually occur because a witch or a wizard casts a spell on a prince or princess, and the spell is usually broken through the efforts of the hero. That common theme runs through "The Calf with the Golden Horns" which also illustrates a very common motif: that of the "Obstacle Flight" in which objects are thrown behind those who are fleeing to delay a pursuer. Probably the best known tale on this theme is the Greek myth of the golden apples that Hippomenes threw before Atalanta so he might win the race.

In many French-Canadian tales the hero is Ti-Jean—little John—the French-Canadian counterpart of the Jack of the Jack tales so popular in Anglo-American tradition. "Ti-Jean and the White Cat" is a good example of this large group. It also features a transformation—the cat is a princess—and it illustrates the three quests so often set as trials for the hero, as well as the usual triumph of the youngest son.

Ghost stories are often legends that are believed, but ghosts may also turn up in fictional tales like "Fearless Pierre." Although this is clearly not told as a true story, it does illustrate many of the beliefs associated with ghosts: that they can't rest in their graves if they are buried without proper funeral rites; that a murdered person cannot rest until his murderer is discovered; that the dead can return to guide the living to buried treasure; and that ghosts can be laid by religious ceremonies.

Although folktales normally end with the triumph of the hero or heroine who is to live happily ever after, sometimes they also emphasize the punishment of the wicked, and that becomes the main theme in a small group that illustrate the belief that crime is always revealed. In one of the most famous tales on this theme, part of a murdered person's body is made into a musical instrument which then reveals the murder. In English tradition the best known form is the ballad of "The Twa Sisters," and, in Europe, it is usually a man who murders his brother. But, French-Canadian versions tell of a little boy cutting off his little sister's finger. In the short tale of "Poucet and Marie" the child is not actually killed, but a longer form of the same story, "Le Petit Doigt enchanté," conforms more closely to the usual plot. It is interesting to note that there is also a cycle of tales about "Petit Poucet" in which the hero is usually good or clever; here he is definitely a bad and stupid little boy.

When we turn from the "Tales of Magic" to the "Romantic Tales," the plots are somewhat more realistic. "The Three Golden Hairs" is an example of one very old and very widespread plot in this category. It features a husband who makes a wager that his wife will remain chaste and a villain who produces false proofs that he has seduced her. Boccaccio used this plot in one of his stories, and in English it is best known through Shakespeare's Cymbeline.

One of the most universal of all folktales tells of a ruler who poses riddles that one of his subjects must answer on pain of death. Its most common English form is "King John and the Abbot of Canterbury" which exists both as a tale and as a ballad. Walter Anderson analyzed nearly six hundred versions from practically every European country in a book that Stith Thompson described as "probably the most exhaustive study ever made of a folktale." The French-Canadian version, "The Carefree Miller," is unusual. Unlike most versions which centre on the riddling session, the miller's plight becomes incidental to the adventures of Ti-Jean which begin with a quite separate episode. This also illustrates the tendency of the folk to portray their heroes as two-sided: Ti-Jean is usually the brave and clever youngest son who triumphs over all obstacles, but here he is a clever but naughty fellow who redeems himself in the end.

The last two stories in this section are both based on the idea that the Devil carries out his search for souls by making bargains with humans. This of course is a widespread theme that turns up in many tales both folk and literary, most focusing on the device by which the Devil is thwarted. "The Devil and the Candle" incorporates two common motifs: the Devil is promised "the first thing you meet" which turns out to be the child instead of the dog the man expected. This device is reversed in another folk tale, "The Dog on the Bridge," where the Devil is promised the first living thing to cross the bridge, expecting a human, and is forced to accept a dog. The device of getting the Devil to agree to wait until the candle burns out is an ancient theme that turns up in the Greek myth of Meleager: at his birth a prophesy said he would die when a certain log was burned, but his mother hid the log.

In "The Split Tuque" the Devil is cheated of his promised soul by the ingenuity of the hero. The device of setting the Devil an impossible task occurs in many tales, but here the use of a Canadian farm setting and a typical article of clothing localizes the story nicely.

3   The Calf with the Golden Horns

Once upon a time there was a man who was a widower, and he had a young son. When the boy had reached the age of twelve or thirteen his father remarried a wicked old witch who spent her time doing all kinds of cruel things to her stepson. By what tricks the old witch managed to wheedle the father, who until then had enjoyed a quiet life, nobody could explain or understand.

The father soon saw that his wife made his young son suffer. He asked her to be good to him and for his part he bought all kinds of things to amuse him. But as soon as he bought the toys the old witch made them disappear.

One day he came home leading a beautiful little calf with golden horns. You can imagine the child's transports of joy. The old witch was also pleased for she knew that this little calf with the golden horns was a handsome prince who had been bewitched by a jealous young fairy. As she herself had loved him, she resolved to make him suffer or disappear. She had another good reason: the prince wanted to marry the king's pretty daughter.

As the witch was hated by the fine people of the court she began to beat and starve the calf. Then she decided to bury it alive. But she dug hole after hole and none was deep enough. The golden horns of the little calf always showed above ground. She worked for a long time to make them disappear but, as they always came up to the surface, she gave up the task.

When the child realized that his little calf with the golden horns had disappeared, he asked about it. Receiving no satisfactory response, he wept for a long time; then he started to search for it. Soon he saw something shining in the sun. As he approached he saw the two golden horns of his little calf. Quickly he started to shovel the earth out, managing to uncover his little calf and get it out of the hole. He was none too soon, for it was almost dead. But, when he rubbed it down he restored it to life and soon the little calf was on its feet as strong as ever.

The boy was delighted to have recovered his little calf with the golden horns, but what was his surprise to hear it speak and say to him: "My dear little boy, you're very good to me, but if you wish to save my life you must get on my back and ride away from here."

"But what will my father think, who is so good to both of us?"

"Don't worry. I'll bring you back later, but if we don't run away now the old witch will kill both of us. Hurry, for if the witch finds us she'll destroy us this very night."

Without replying the boy climbed on his little calf and they set out. They travelled the rest of that day and all through the night without stopping. The next morning at daybreak when they were going to rest, the little calf suddenly said to the boy: "Don't you see something coming?"

"Yes," said the little boy, "and I recognize the old witch. She's chasing us, and I'm afraid she'll catch us soon for she's taken the fastest horse in my father's stable."

"Get on my back and let us flee as fast as my feet let me, and you must do everything I tell you."

After running some time the boy said: "The old witch is going to catch us soon for her horse runs like the wind."

"My little friend, I'm going to ask you to do something you'll hate to do, but it's necessary for our safety. Cut off one of my golden horns and throw it behind us. Hurry, for if you let the witch get too close it'll be the death of both of us."

The boy did with regret what his little calf told him to do, and when he threw the golden horn he was astonished to see a mountain spring up. The golden horn fell with its point up. It turned into a mountain bristling with such dangerous peaks that the horse stopped and refused to go any further. The old witch decided to go around the mountain, hoping that the speed of her horse would make up for lost time.

The little calf kept on going as fast as it could until the little boy cried suddenly: "The old witch is again on our heels."

"My little friend, when you see that she comes too close, in spite of the sorrow you feel cut off my other golden horn and throw it behind you."

Again, in spite of his sorrow, when the little boy judged that the old witch was close enough, he cut off the last horn and threw it behind him. This time the horn fell with its point down, and as it entered the earth it made a large deep lake.

It was just in time. The old witch, about to overtake the fugitives, came on with a dizzy speed so that she hadn't time to stop her horse. They were both engulfed in the lake and drowned.

At the same moment the little calf, stripped of his golden horns which were the witchcraft keeping him in the form of an animal, recovered his own shape of the young prince. Overjoyed, he took the road to the king's castle, accompanied by the little boy.

All the people were happy over the young prince's return for they had been very worried by his long absence. The young princess, especially, was so happy that they decided to have the wedding immediately. A few years later the boy who had helped the prince also married a young princess.

The wicked fairy, more jealous and angry than ever, slipped into the castle in the shape of a little white cat. But the king's big dog, seeing her as she came in, threw himself on her and killed her with a single snap of his jaws.

4 Ti-Jean and The Big White Cat

There is a king who has three sons. One is called Jean, another, Cordon-bleu, and the other, Cordon-vert. One day the king says to them: "All three of you are now of age. The one who will fetch the finest horse will have my crown."

The boys rig themselves up, go out and walk . . . When they reach the fork of three roads Cordon-vert says: "I take this road." Cordon-bleu adds: "And I, this road," and Ti-Jean finishes: "And I the other road." Before separating they agree: "On a certain day we will all return to the fork of the roads."

My Ti-Jean walks and walks right to the end of the road. There he takes a little path into the forest and walks. Arriving near a little straw hut, he sees a big white cat drawing water with four toads. He sits down and watches. The cat, having filled a tank with water, unhitches her four toads and *rrnyao, rrnyao*, dips herself in it.

And from the tank comes a fine princess, such as Ti-Jean has never seen. She asks him: "What are you looking for?" "A horse," replies he; "we are three brothers, and our father the king has promised his crown to the one who leads back the finest horse." The princess tells him: "Tomorrow morning I will again be the big white cat that you have seen. You will go into my stable and take the finest of my toads. When you return to your father's you will harness him and the next day he will become the finest horse in the land."

Just like that, the next morning Ti-Jean takes the toad and rides it away *patati, patata*. At the three roads he meets his brothers whose horses are very fine. Looking at Ti-Jean and his toad they say: "Don't show yourself like that to our father or you'll kill yourself." But he comes behind them, *patati, patata*, whipping his mount with a little willow switch. "Don't come with us," they say, "it's a real disgrace." "That doesn't matter, let's go."

They arrive at their father's late in the day and put their horses in the stable. Ti-Jean uses the comb on his toad, *perarrar*. And his brothers say: "You're going to break our father's comb." "Papa can afford another one."

The next morning Cordon-bleu and Cordon-vert rise and go to show their fine horses to the king. "And Ti-Jean?" he asks.

They reply: "Oh, him? He has a toad." "A toad? I must see it." Ti-Jean rises after the others. His toad is the finest horse that has ever been seen, with a silver mane and golden shoes. "Ah!" cries the king, "it's Ti-Jean who has won, he has the finest horse. But you know that a king has three tests. Now the one of you who will bring me the finest hand-woven cloth will have my crown." And the three go out on their horses.

Reaching the fork of the three roads, Cordon-bleu says: "I take the same road." Cordon-vert also takes the same. "I also take mine," finishes Ti-Jean, and sets out.

He walks and walks, reaches the little path, and from there to the little house covered with straw. The big white cat is still drawing water with her three toads. Ti-Jean sits down and watches them do it.

Once the tank is full, rrnyao, rrnyao, the white cat dips herself in the tank and comes out a fine princess. She says: "This time, my Ti-Jean, what are you looking for?" He replies: "I'm looking for the finest homespun that my father has ever seen." "Tomorrow morning," replies the princess, "I'll again become a big white cat. You will look in my small chest of drawers and you will take the ugliest walnut that you find there and put it in your pocket. When you reach your father's you will slit it with a knife and it will become thirty ells of the finest cloth ever seen."

Cordon-bleu and Cordon-vert met at the three roads. Oh, what fine cloth they have! But Ti-Jean, having put the nut in his pocket, has nothing. One of his brothers asks him: "Ti-Jean, I think you have nothing?" To which he replies, "I think that with all the cloth you have, my father will have enough."

At their father the king's next morning, they rise and go to show their cloth. Their cloth is beautiful. That of Cordon-vert especially is unequalled. "As for Ti-Jean, I think he has nothing." But Ti-Jean arrives and gives the nut to his father, saying: "Split this on the table with a knife." The king splits the nut and it becomes thirty ells of the finest cloth that he has ever seen. He says: "It's Ti-Jean who has won again. But you know a king has three tests. Next there remains still one thing to do." "What is that?" they ask. "The one who will fetch the most beautiful woman will have my crown, and this time, it is the end."

They all go out again, Cordon-vert and Cordon-bleu on their horses and Ti-Jean on his toad. Cordon-bleu says: "I'll take the same road again." Cordon-vert: "And me too." And Ti-Jean: "I also take mine."

He walks and walks, and Ti-Jean reaches the little hut covered with straw, and sees again the big white cat drawing water with her toads.

Rrnyao, rrnyao, the cat plunges into the tank full of water and comes out a beautiful princess. Ti-Jean falls on his back with admiration, so beautiful does he find her. "Tell me then, Ti-Jean, what are you looking for on your third trip here?" And he replies: "You know my father the king has three tests. He has said, 'The one who brings me the most beautiful girl, it's the last, he will have my crown.'" And he adds: "Now I have never seen on this earth one more beautiful than you." She says: "I am transformed, and I will become a princess again only if the king's son marries me." Ti-Jean says, "Good!" "Tomorrow morning," adds she, "I will again be a big white cat. You will hitch my four toads to my carriage, and we will go together."

The next morning, Ti-Jean rises and sees the princess transformed. He hitches the toads to the carriage and seats himself on the small seat, the big white cat beside him. In this way she brushes against him, walks on his knees, and rubs her cheeks against his, rrnyao, rrnyao!

His brothers reach the fork of the three roads. By God, they have beautiful girls! Then they look at Ti-Jean with his white cat and the four toads and say: "That's the limit. Ti-Jean is going to kill himself." And they are delighted. "With that old carriage and those four toads, he's nothing to us." "Let's go, then," replies he.

There he is behind them, whipping the toads with a switch, while the white cat brushes against his face mewing rrnyao, rrnyao. The three brothers reach their father's, Ti-Jean leads the white cat into his room and goes to brush his toads, bring, brang, brang! "Ti-Jean, you're going to break your father's comb." "Our father can get another."

In the morning the king finds that Cordon-vert and Cordon-bleu have some beautiful girls. He asks: "Ti-Jean?" "Oh, he has a big white cat." "Be that as it may, I must see her." And my

Ti-Jean comes in holding his princess by the hand. It isn't that the king can't believe it, he has never seen so beautiful a girl in his life.

Having hitched the toads, Ti-Jean arrives with four un-equalled horses and a carriage such as no one has ever seen. The three brothers go away together to marry their girls, Ti-Jean marrying the princess.

"It's my Ti-Jean who has won my crown," says the king, and, raising it from his head, bang, he puts it on Ti-Jean's head.

And so it goes . . . I was at the wedding. But since then, I haven't seen those people, and I don't know how things go over there.

5 Fearless Pierre

Once there was a widow who lived on the edge of a forest, working as a cobbler for the village folk. She had only one little boy who was called Pierre. It was he who went to look for work for his mother in the village. When she had mended the shoes he delivered them.

They had nicknamed this little boy Fearless Pierre because he was never afraid. Everyone in the village had tried to scare him in all kinds of ways, but they were never able to do so.

To keep it short, when Fearless Pierre was bigger and when he noticed that his mother was supporting him he said to her one day, "I know the trade of shoemaking like you. Now I'll go to earn my living, and at the same time help you a little." The widow didn't want to hear him speak of this. It was strange to see her little Pierre leaving.

But Pierre wanted to go at any cost. One fine morning, willy-nilly, well equipped with underclothes, he said goodbye to his mother and away he went. He walked for eight days. At the end of that time he reached the edge of a forest where he built himself a kind of little shack and started to work at shoemaking. There was a group of hunters who passed that way. Sometimes Pierre had a chance to fix their boots, but he didn't earn much.

He was in the forest for seven or eight years, and he had reached the age of twenty-two when the king's Grand Vizier went hunting. Passing through the underbrush he had scraped one of his boots, then he chanced to pass right in front of Fearless Pierre's shack.

"Young man, will you fix my boots?" "Yes, sir."

The king's Grand Vizier watched him while he was waiting for his boots. After they were fixed he took a golden coin and gave it to him saying, "Young man, it seems to me your place in the forest isn't the right location for mending shoes. A hunter passes only every three or four months. It seems to me that if you enlisted as a king's soldier you'd make a better living."

"Sir, I'm all right. I earn my living as I can."

"Young man, is it fear that keeps you from enlisting as a soldier?"

"No, sir, I've never known fear in my life."

"Is it true that you've never known fear in your life?"

"Yes, it's indeed true. I've never known fear in my life."

The king's Grand Vizier said then: "If I knew that you spoke the truth your fortune would be made."

"I assure you that I speak the truth."

"If I come to find you to try to prove that you've never known fear, will you come?"

"Yes, sir, I'll come."

"What are you called?"

"I'm called Fearless Pierre."

The Grand Vizier left and went to the king. When he reached the king's castle the king called his council together for a special session. "Sire, my king, I've found the man we've looked for for a long time."

The king lived in a castle. He had moved out of his father's castle seven years ago because he couldn't stay there. Every evening there was an uproar in the old castle, everyone became afraid, and was forced to get out. The king had issued a proclamation throughout his kingdom that if anyone would rid him of whoever caused the uproar, he'd give him a great reward. Several attempted it but by midnight they'd all been forced to run away. That made the king build another castle a couple of arpents away from the old one, and he stayed there with his staff.

The Grand Vizier said, "Sire, my king, you have issued a proclamation to find a person who would sleep in the old castle and tell you the next morning who it is that caused this uproar."

"Yes, Grand Vizier."

"Well, sire, I've found one."

"Grand Vizier, if you speak the truth, I want this man to come and sleep in my castle this evening."

The Grand Vizier had two horses saddled, mounted one, took the other by the bridle, and went to look for Fearless Pierre. He wouldn't leave without taking his tools with him. This was because he thought they'd sent for him to work at his trade.

Arriving at the castle, the Grand Vizier presented Fearless Pierre to the king and said, "Fearless Pierre, this is my king. Arrange everything with him for the orders he's going to give you for the evening."

The king said, "Young man, do you see that castle over there, eh? It's seven years since we left, it was impossible to stay there. We heard all sorts of noise and no one has been able to stay there after sunset. Can you sleep there for a night? Are you afraid?"

"No, sir, I'm never afraid."

"What do you need to pass the night?"

Fearless Pierre, who liked drinking, told him, "Sire, my king, I'd very much like a couple of bottles of rum, and if I had some old pairs of shoes I could mend them while waiting for those who are going to appear."

"On my word what you ask for you will have."

The bottles of rum were brought, three or four old pairs of shoes also, and Fearless Pierre took the road to the castle. The first thing he did was close all the doors and windows and start to drink. When he was very tipsy and hardly able to walk, he went to sleep on a couch and slept right to eleven o'clock in the evening . . . . When he woke he thought, "If someone happens to come and I'm forced to fight, I'd indeed be in a bad state, drunk as I am."

He got up, took a chair, and started to mend the shoes the king had given him, He found this didn't work and lay down again. Right at midnight he heard the great door of the castle open and saw four men enter carrying a coffin. They put the coffin on the ground and began to sing in a circle. Fearless Pierre said to himself, "Is this what drove out the king's attendants? Is this what scared the others?"

He crawled toward them. Seeing him come the four men who had brought the coffin went out the door and left the coffin there. That sobered Fearless Pierre up a bit. He started to work on the shoes. While working he began to whistle. But there was a man lying in the coffin and he said, "When one watches the dead, one doesn't whistle."

Fearless Pierre jumped, but he replied, "When one is dead one doesn't speak, and if you don't close your mouth I'll close it for you very soon."

Fearless Pierre again began to work and to whistle, and for the second time the dead man said to him, "When one watches the dead one doesn't whistle."

"When one is dead one doesn't chatter." He took his shoe and grabbed the fellow by the hair and gave him three or four blows on the head with the shoe, saying: "If you weren't dead already you will be shortly." It goes without saying that the one who was lying in the coffin didn't stir. Fearless Pierre continued to mend his shoes, even going to find his bottle and taking a drink.

He thought perhaps the fellow who was lying there would like a drink if he wasn't dead. "Partner, do you want a drink?" It goes without saying that the other didn't speak. He caught him by the hair and seated him in the coffin and said, "Come take a drink with me."

"Listen, young man, give me your hand, then get me out of the coffin."

Pierre took hold of him under the arms and put him on the floor. "Young man, light a candle and open that door there." It was the door of the cellar. They both went down into the cellar. Pierre held the dead man under the arms. Reaching the back of the cellar he found a pickaxe and the dead man said, "Dig, young man, dig here." Fearless Pierre dug. Suddenly it rang as you might say like metal. Fearless Pierre, who was as strong as two ordinary men, took out a pail of gold. The dead man said, "This pail of gold is for my son. Dig a little farther."

Fearless Pierre dug and brought out still another pail also full of gold. The dead man said, "That is for my daughter. Now dig in this corner here." Fearless Pierre dug in the corner indicated and brought out a pail equally rich full of silver. The dead man said, "That one is for you, young man."

Then he said, "Early tomorrow morning you are going to the castle. You don't know my son or daughter. My son is the king and the girl who lives with him is my daughter. You'll tell the king that I was murdered seven years ago and my body was buried under an apple tree in the garden behind the castle. You'll tell him also that he must dig up my bones, bury them in holy ground, and have a service sung for me. Then he can live in this castle when he likes, he'll hear nothing. It needed a brave young man like you to free me."

"That is all?"

"Yes, that is all." He disappeared into the air in front of Fearless Pierre.

Fearless Pierre climbed upstairs, very pleased to have seen all this, and said, "I can take a drink now."

Next morning at daybreak Fearless Pierre opened all the windows and doors, then strode out on the porch. The king rose early to see if his man had fled like the others. His biggest surprise was to see Fearless Pierre striding on the porch and smoking. The king took four of his servants to conduct him to the castle; he couldn't go alone, he was too frightened.

Arriving there he said to Fearless Pierre: "Good day, young man."

"Good day, sire, my king. I've passed the night quite well. Only there came four frightful ones, some kind of fools, with a coffin. In this coffin they had a man lying down who seemed dead. But he wasn't. I spoke to him and he told me he was your father."

"Young man," said the king, "my father died seven years ago when I was young."

"Well, then, sire, my king, come and see."

The king went down into the cellar with Fearless Pierre and Pierre said, "Sire, my king, that pail of gold there is for you, the other is for your sister, and that one is for me. Your father told me he was murdered seven years ago."

"That's right. He disappeared at that time."

"Well, he's buried under an apple tree in the corner of the garden behind the castle. He told me to tell you to dig up his bones, to bury them in holy ground, and have a service sung for him. After that you can stay in the castle when you wish, you'll never hear anything."

It hardly needs saying that the king didn't hesitate. He took some men immediately, went directly under the apple tree, found the bones, and buried them in holy ground, then had a service sung for his father.

Fearless Pierre was a fine boy of twenty-two or twenty-three, quite intelligent even though he had had no education. After the service he'd rendered the king, seeing that he was so brave, the king said to his sister, "Why don't you marry this Fearless Pierre? He isn't ugly, he isn't stupid, you could do something with him." The young princess didn't dislike Pierre at all. The king said to Pierre, "How would you like to marry my sister? She is rich and pretty. How will it suit you to marry her?"

Fearless Pierre married the princess and when I passed by there the last time they were still living.

6   Poucet and Marie

Poucet and Marie were two children who lived happily with their parents. One day, when their mother suffered from a bad cold, the two little ones went out to go by themselves to the first village to buy some medicine for their mother. They hurried to the store and, after buying some lozenges for their mother, set out for home.

On the road they amused themselves by picking flowers and gathering nuts. Poucet, seeing that his sister had more than he, wanted her to share with him. Marie gave him some nuts, but Poucet was angry, and to punish Marie for not giving him as many as she had, he cut off the little finger of her right hand. Then seeing that his sister cried and grew weak from the pain, he hid her under a pile of branches and returned to the house alone, taking Marie's little finger with him.

When Poucet arrived home, his anxious mother wanted to know where his little sister was. Poucet told her that Marie had cut off her little finger and was dead of fright. But how astonished was Poucet to hear the little finger speak!

The mother, learning of her little son's wickedness, took him to the place where Marie was and, for punishment, he had to stay under the pile of branches in his turn, while Marie returned with her mother.

A little while afterwards the wolves found and ate the wicked Poucet.

7   The Three Golden Hairs

Once upon a time, let me tell you, there was a prince. One day he married a princess, the daughter of another king—princes always married their own kind.

One fine morning the prince said he was going on a trip to a foreign land to buy some merchandise and silk goods. Who came to see him? The lord of the town. "Where are you going, your highness? You've just got married and you're already going to travel to a foreign country?"

"Yes, I have to make this trip."

"Will you bet with me that I'll win the princess's favours before you return from your trip?"

"Yes, by George, I'll bet against that. If you win favours from my princess before my return, you'll have all my goods; if you don't, I'll have yours."

The prince gone, the lord went that evening to see the princess. Once, in passing, he stole a garter from her chair. When he returned the next morning, "Look, your lordship," said the princess, "You come here very often. You can stay at home, I don't need you here." The lord went with hardly any shame and stole one of the princess's nightdresses that hung on a line in the courtyard.

Next day he dressed his maid servant as a beggar and sent her with a basket to beg her bread at the palace. The beggar asked to stay the night. They put her up.

At the end of the evening the princess retired to her room, undressed, and took off her rings which she put in a drawer of the dressing table. In the corner in the darkness the beggar watched and saw everything she did. The beautiful princess had three golden hairs on her left shoulder. As soon as she was asleep the servant approached on tiptoe, stole the rings from the dressing-table drawer, pulled out the three golden hairs, and returned to the lord, her master.

"Here," she said, "Here are the three golden hairs that she had on her left shoulder, and here are the rings that she put in her dressing-table drawer before going to bed."

"I thank you very much, my girl, that's what I needed."

The prince returned from his journey. As he left his ship the lord came to meet him. "Tell me," he said, "How was your trip?"

"My trip was fine."

The lord began again: "But it wasn't so fine here. I have had some favours from the princess before your return."

"What have you had?"

"I've had her garter."

"You've had her garter—oh, you could have stolen it from her chair in the castle."

"But that's not all. Here's her nightdress that she gave me."

"Oh, her nightdress. You could have stolen it when she hung her washing on the line."

"But that's not all. I have her rings."

"Oh, you haven't yet won my goods. It needs more than that."

"But I have still more. Do you know these three golden hairs that she had on her left shoulder?"

The prince turned back and went to find his wife. He said, "My wife, get dressed. I've lost everything." He set out with his wife in a small boat and went to sea. In the middle of the sea he threw his wife into the water and went away. The princess wasn't drowned. Her clothes made her float on the water. That's how she reached land. On land she went into a city and there she dressed like a lawyer.

The prince walked and walked, right to the ends of the earth.

After a long time he reached the city where his wife was. But he didn't recognize her when they met. She asked him, "Sir, where are you going?"

"Where am I going? I'm walking to the ends of the earth."

"But you must have done something terrible to walk to the ends of the earth?"

"Ah, yes. I wagered goods against goods with a lord that he wouldn't gain favours from my princess before my return from a trip. When I came back he showed me her garter, he showed me her nightdress. I said, 'You could have taken them yourself from the chair and from the line.' He showed me her rings and he showed me the three golden hairs that she had on her left shoulder."

"Well, sir," she said, "you wagered goods against goods with him. What will you give me if I plead your case and win it?" As a lawyer she was going to appear before a judge to sue the lord.

When the lord was in court under oath the lawyer asked him, "Didn't you steal this garter from the chair?"

"Yes, I stole the garter from a chair."

"You also stole the nightdress from the line where it was hanging."

"Yes."

"You sent your servant dressed as a beggar to ask lodging at the castle."

"Yes."

"Didn't she steal the rings from the dressing table?"

"Yes."

"While the princess slept didn't she pull out the three golden hairs from her left shoulder?"

"Yes."

"Your Honour, you have taken note of this. You know what I mean—that the lord has lost his goods, Your Honour." It's the woman lawyer who pleaded his just cause. She turned to the prince her husband and she asked, "Will you recognize your wife if you see her?"

He replied, "Yes, I'd recognize her."

The lawyer without losing an instant went into a nearby room. From the room the princess his wife came out and said, "Do you recognize me, my husband?"

"Oh, yes, I recognize you, my wife." She grabbed her husband around the neck and gave him a big kiss there before everybody.

The judge said, "Your highness, you've won all the lord's goods, and I condemn him."

The prince went with his wife the princess to his castle where they have lived happily ever since. As for the lord, he was sent to walk to the ends of the earth in his turn, and he's walking still.

8   The Carefree Miller

Once there was an old man and his wife who lived happily in
ease and contentment, without worry about their old age. Their
only concern centred on their boy Ti-Jean, who was intelligent
but also very resourceful and hot-tempered. It was this last
fault that worried them most.

One evening the father had returned from the city with a big
turkey and goose. He said, "Ti-Jean, I'm giving you this goose
because you've been good today. Take good care of it." Ti-Jean
who was eight or nine then was pleased by his father's attention and resolved to take care of the goose as he'd been told.

Some time later Ti-Jean was uneasy. The goose disappeared
and then returned without anyone finding where it had gone.
One day when he'd gone to look for it, he suddenly heard a
loud noise. Looking in the direction of the noise he saw the big
turkey beating its wings, pecking at something, and crying
loudly, "You'll die of it! You'll die of it!" Ti-Jean ran up and
what did he see? His goose stretched out dead on a nest of eggs
and the turkey attacking her, pecking her on the head and crying louder and louder, "You'll die of it! You'll die of it!"

At the sight Ti-Jean, believing that the big turkey had killed
his goose, became very angry. Seizing a heavy club he beat at
the turkey which gave its last "You'll die of it!" and sank down
dead itself. That gave Ti-Jean's father and mother still another
reason to worry over his temper tantrums.

However, Ti-Jean was incorrigible and also, as he grew up,
he became very dishonest. One of Ti-Jean's father's many occu-
pations was that of raising and fattening pigs. He always had a
large flock in a pen near a bog which was very deep. One day
the father and mother went to town. The father gave Ti-Jean
strict orders to take good care of the pigs, especially to be careful to keep the gate closed because of the danger that the pigs
would sink in the bog nearby.

His father and mother had scarcely been gone half an hour
when an animal buyer came to Ti-Jean asking if the large flock
of pigs he'd seen in the pen were for sale. Ti-Jean refused at
first but the buyer persisted and offered him a good price so he
finally decided to sell but on condition that he, Ti-Jean, cut and
kept the tails of the pigs. The buyer agreed. Ti-Jean cut the tail

off each pig and put the pigs in the cart of the merchant who soon disappeared with his purchase.

As soon as he'd gone Ti-Jean went to put the pigs' tails in the bog, opened the gate, and went to work. At suppertime his father came and saw the gate was open and his pigs gone. He questioned Ti-Jean but the wicked rascal said that he didn't know who had opened the gate. All he could say was that the pigs had all disappeared into the bog when he saw their tails on the surface.

Making Ti-Jean see what a disaster he'd caused, his father ordered him to pull the drowned pigs out by the tails. Perhaps by washing and bleeding them he could save a good part of the meat. With the aid of some planks Ti-Jean made a kind of floating bridge to get near the tails. Then with contortions and grimaces he pretended to try to pull the pigs out of the slough. Suddenly he seized one cut tail, pretended to fall, and upset. Then having frightened his father, Ti-Jean threw away the tails he'd caught, pretending to be in despair at not being able to succeed in his task. His father became disheartened over the loss of his pigs and scolded Ti-Jean for the rest of the night.

The next day, when his father and mother got up, Ti-Jean had disappeared. During the night he'd got up quietly, made a bundle of clothes and food, and taken to the road, determined never to return to his parents' home. His pocket well-filled with the money from the sale of the pigs, he walked for three days till he came to a flour mill where he stopped to rest. The miller, who needed a man, offered to hire him. Ti-Jean accepted immediately, for this miller had the reputation of never knowing anxiety. He was always good-humoured, without worry or trouble—they called him the carefree miller.

Three months later a surprising event happened. The king had long heard of this miller, reputed never to have known anxiety. One day the king was guided to his place and after a long conversation he said to him, "Miller, our positions in life are not equal. In spite of your poverty you have a happy life without anxiety; me, in spite of glory and grandeur, I am tired out by worries, troubles of all sorts. I want to know if you can take part of them. Three days from now you'll have to tell me three things. Where is the centre of the earth? How much I am worth, and what I think. If you can't answer these three questions it will be the worse for you."

On these last words the king went away, leaving the miller perplexed and thinking hard. The more time passed the more thoughtful and worried the miller became. Ti-Jean noticed the change in the miller's mood and asked the reason. When the miller told him the reason for his anxiety, Ti-Jean, who somewhat resembled the miller, offered to go to see the king in his place. The miller accepted the proposal immediately, and the next day Ti-Jean, dressed in the miller's clothes, went to the King's palace, and was brought into his presence.

"Well, miller, can you tell me where the centre of the world is?"

"Sire, my king," replied Ti-Jean, "The centre of the world is where Your Majesty puts his feet."

The king, put in good humour by this reply, smiled and said, "I'll accept that, but now tell me how much I am worth."

"Sire, my king, Your Majesty is worth twenty-nine pieces of silver."

"What!" said the king, startled. "Only twenty-nine pieces of silver? Explain that to me."

"Sire, my king, our Lord was sold for thirty pieces of silver. He was certainly worth one piece more than you."

"Bravo!" said the king, "I accept that also. Tell me now what I am thinking."

"Sire, my king, you think you're speaking to the miller, but you're speaking to Ti-Jean, his hired man."

The king, satisfied with Ti-Jean's answers, hired him to live in the castle and gave him the highest posts awarded to any servant. Later Ti-Jean went to visit his old parents whom he found living almost in poverty. He was forgiven his past escapades and saw that they lived out their days in contentment and happiness.

9   The Split Tuque

Jacques Russot was a man of fifty. He had formerly owned considerable wealth in lands, herds of horned animals, and especially silver. He'd been renowned for his skill in making profitable bargains; when he went to the market with his herds of fat animals he always returned with a pocket well filled with jingling coins of gold or silver.

At the time this story begins, everything was changed, and Jacques, who had suffered misfortune on misfortune, like Job, was reduced to black misery, and his distress was painful to see. Late in the fall when all his crops were in the barn, one night a thunderbolt fell on his buildings and reduced everything to ashes. That wasn't all. The fire spread to his stables and all his fine fat animals perished in the flames. For the height of misfortune, in the winter that followed a new fire consumed his house while all his family were in a deep sleep. His wife and children perished and Jacques alone was able to save himself with great difficulty. He became depressed by this last misfortune and abandoned himself to despair, even uttering the most senseless curses.

The Devil appeared to Jacques and said to him, "Jacques Russot, I've heard your lamentations and I've come to propose a bargain. If you'll sign a paper that you'll belong to me body and soul in a year and a day, I promise to give you all kinds of gold and silver and pleasures from now until the time is expired."

Before the apparition Jacques stood quite dumbfounded, but he soon recovered from his agitation. His cunning instinct for making bargains getting the upper hand, he looked at the Devil fixedly and replied, "I don't know what to do with all the gold and silver you can get for me. However, I'll sign a paper pledging to belong to you at the end of a year and a day on three conditions. First, you will fill my tuque with gold and silver; second, I will drill a hole at the top of my barn, I'll nail my tuque inside, and it will be through that hole that you will fill it, and finally the third condition, which comes to the same thing, you promise me not to show yourself here for a year and a day so that I may enjoy in peace the silver that you'll have poured into my tuque."

"Agreed," said the Devil, smiling. "And when will we begin?"

"Tomorrow at nine o'clock in the morning," replied Jacques Russot.

The Devil left grinning, and Jacques watched him go smiling; both seemed satisfied with their bargains.

The next day at daybreak Jacques went to bore a little hole in the roof of his barn; inside opposite a big hay press he nailed his tuque, after he'd carefully unstitched the bottom of it. He had also inserted two strings in the sack so he could open or close the bottom as he wished.

At nine o'clock the Devil arrived with two sacks of silver under his arm, climbed on the roof of the barn, and poured the contents into the little hole. What was his surprise to realize that his two sacks weren't enough to fill the tuque. He put his hand through the little hole—the tuque was indeed there but empty.

He climbed down to find six sacks of silver and climbed back to pour them into the tuque. He put his hand in, the tuque was always there, but always empty. Jacques was in the barn working his strings. When the Devil poured in the silver he loosened the string and the silver slipped through the split bottom of the tuque to fall in the centre of the hay press. The Devil carried his sacks of silver all day and the tuque was still not full.

The next day he began again, but strangely enough the tuque was never filled. The Devil began to think that it could well be some trick of Jacques for several times during the day he'd heard him humming a verse that seemed to make fun of him:

> You're a good devil, you're a good devil.
> Pour, pour into my tuque.
> Look, search, and covet.
> It's a good devil, it's a good devil.
> These fine coins, these fine coins,
> Yes, from my tuque they've vanished.

Jacques had reason to sing for the poured silver passed through the tuque and fell into the hay press, which was nearly half filled.

The next day the Devil began to carry his sacks of silver, but seeing that the tuque was no more full than the day before he began to storm and to threaten Jacques that he'd go to see what was happening in the barn. But Jacques warned him that if he showed himself to him he'd have broken his bargain. The Devil made still more trips, finally flying into a great rage, and gave up the contest, hurling curses and raging over being tricked by Jacques Russot. He went away breathing so much fire and smoke that he nearly set fire to the buildings. Jacques watched him leave, rubbing his hands with great satisfaction. He hummed:

> He's a good devil, he's a good devil.
> Your fine coins, your fine coins
> For me are not disappearing.

Jacques Russot lived several years very peacefully and kept busy giving charity to the poor. The trick played on the Devil was his last bargain.

10   The Devil and the Candle

Once upon a time there was a man, his wife, and their little boy. The man went fishing every day but he never caught a fish.

"It's useless to go fishing," his wife says to him one day. "You never catch anything. You'd do better to try to get a job instead of letting us starve."

But he replies, "Fishing, it's my trade. I'm not able to get a job and I won't do it."

The next morning he goes out to fish as usual, in spite of his wife's reproaches. As he fishes, a man suddenly appears on the river.

"What are you doing, my friend?"

"I'm fishing. I never catch anything. It's very strange."

"Do you want to catch some fish?" the fellow asks him.

"Why, it's my trade—that's the reason I want to catch them."

"Well, if you're willing to give me whatever comes to meet you, your boat will be filled with fish."

The fisherman says to himself, "That's not a big thing, what's coming to meet me is my little black dog." To the other he cries: "That's fine. You'll have whatever comes to meet me." Then in one moment he catches so many fish that his boat is filled.

But instead of his little black dog, it's his little boy who comes to meet him. Fear seizes the child at the sight of the stranger, the Devil in person. As he had to cross a wood, the child traced a great circle in the sand, made some little crosses all around, and got in the middle.

Seeing that he's promised his child to the Devil, the fisherman is very downhearted and doesn't know what to do. But his wife says to him, "Come on, then, we must play a trick on him. When is he coming?"

"Tomorrow."

The next day the Devil arrives. "You see the candle that I've lighted?" the wife asks him. "Will you leave me my child until it burns itself out?"

The Devil replies, "But certainly." And he thinks to himself, "It doesn't make much difference. In a moment this candle will be finished." The candle was scarcely half burned; the woman blew it out. "Now the candle is out, your little boy is mine."

"But no," she replies. "The candle didn't go out by itself, I blew it out."

Thwarted, the Devil was forced to go away with a flea in his ear. The child had been saved.

III Jokes and Anecdotes

The plots involved in the "Ordinary Folktales"—Märchen, fairy tales, "contes populaires"—are usually fairly complicated, involving a series of incidents. The third type, "Jokes and Anecdotes," are much simpler, usually involving only one incident. These are the most familiar kind in the modern world. Tall tales depending on exaggeration for their humour, bawdy jokes, and tales of stupid characters, usually directed against some particular group—Newfoundlanders, Ukrainians, Pakistanis, etc.—are probably the most common forms of folktales told in Canada today. However, the jokes and anecdotes that people have told for many centuries in many countries are much more varied, and many of them have been collected in Canada. The eight that follow represent some of the different types.

"Dalbec Flies through the Air" is a good example of the tall tale: it is one of the many yarns spun by hunters and fishermen about their strange and wonderful exploits. Here of course it is nicely localized with its references to the St. Lawrence and the church at Ste. Anne's.

"The Pumpkin Seller" is one of the large group of tales about fools and their absurd misunderstandings. This particular joke is very widespread: as Thompson notes, "It not only appears in Turkish jestbooks, but is told all over Europe, in much of Asia, and among the mountain whites of Virginia." It has also been told by Iroquois Indians, by Anglo-Canadians in Ontario, and by French Canadians in Quebec. The French-Canadian version is one of the best: usually there is no explanation of why the fool thinks the pumpkin is an ass's (or horse's) egg or why he thinks a rabbit is an ass. Here, the setting makes the mistakes slightly more plausible, if equally ridiculous.

The tale of the cobbler and his stubborn wife is one of a group of stories about married couples which usually focus on their quarrels. This one is known all around the world, and is also told in a popular ballad, "Get Up and Bar the Door."

"The Lousy-Head" is another of the stories about a married couple, usually known as "The Obstinate Wife." There are several versions: sometimes the wife falls into a stream and her husband searches for her upstream, saying she is too obstinate to go with the current; sometimes the couple argue whether something has been cut with a knife or scissors, the man throws his wife into the water, and as she sinks she makes a scissors sign with her fingers; or, as in the French-Canadian form, the wife calls her husband a lousy-head and when he throws her in the stream she makes the sign of cracking a louse as she sinks. This form is widespread in Europe but rare in North America.

"The Two Neighbours" is a somewhat more extended anecdote. In fact the theme of "The Master Thief" often forms part of quite complex tales which resemble Märchen more than simple anecdotes. In the most common form, a man boasts of his skill and is challenged to submit to difficult tests. The French-Canadian form, which focusses on the tricks the thief uses to steal an animal, turns up all over the world and has been noted in over three hundred versions.

The story of "The Calf Sold Three Times" is a famous joke known in practically every country of Europe and in many places throughout the rest of the world. An early form was the "Farce de Maître Patelin," but the French-Canadian version has been nicely localized in Quebec. Its popularity is probably due to the folk's distrust of lawyers and their pleasure at seeing one outwitted by an ordinary fellow.

The story of "Richard's Cards" is not as widely known but it has been popular in French Canada, perhaps because of its religious theme. In addition to the tale, the Acadians told the same incident in a song, "La Chanson des cartes."

"The Dreams of the Hunters" is another very popular and widespread tale. It has been traced back to the twelfth century and is well known throughout Europe and Asia as well as North America. Forty-two versions have been noted in Ireland alone, where the three dreamers are often an Englishman, a Scotsman, and an Irishman. Early versions usually had the dreamers competing for the last loaf of bread, but again the French-Canadian form has been localized, with hunters dreaming about the partridge they shot, and, unlike most versions, their dreams have religious themes, emphasizing the importance of religion in Quebec society.

11   Dalbec Flies Through the Air

It was the morning of the "Toussaint" (All Saints Day) that Dalbec had gone out early, shooting. He had expended all his ammunition and was returning home when he saw a flock of wild ducks swimming about among the timbers of a raft that had gone ashore at the mouth of the river. The water was cold, but Dalbec went into it up to his neck and waded round until he could reach under the logs and get hold of the legs of a duck. When he caught one he pulled it quickly under the water and fastened it to his belt. In this way he secured about a dozen.

All of a sudden he felt a commotion, and before he knew what was happening he found himself raised into the air and carried off. A strong northeasterly gale was blowing and away he went up the St. Lawrence. Just as he passed the church at Ste. Anne he heard the first bell of the mass sound, and he wished he had stayed at home instead of going shooting.

At the rate at which he was going he had not much time to think; but presently he realized that something had got to be done. He reached down and twisted the neck of one of the ducks. That let him down a little and he twisted another. So he kept on until, when he had done with them all, he found himself dropped on the ground in front of the church at Sorel, and heard the second bell of the mass. He had been carried seventy-five miles up the river in just half an hour.

12   The Pumpkin Seller

Near a certain village lived a gardener and his family. One fall when he'd harvested a great many fine yellow pumpkins, he had the idea of selling them.

He set out then with his wagon loaded with vegetables. When he'd gone a great distance from his village he happened to pass the home of a farmer's wife who had no horses. Seeing this man pass, the farmer's wife, quite surprised, asked him what he had in his wagon. The gardener, joking, replied that they were mares' eggs.

The farmer's wife went quickly to consult her husband who bought a big yellow pumpkin. After the gardener had gone, the farmer's wife installed herself near a pile of branches to hatch the strange egg while her husband kept busy in the house.

Three weeks having passed, the old farmer was tired of do-ing the cooking and looking after his house. He went to find his wife who, on her side, was very worn out, and tried to per-suade her to give up brooding. saying she wouldn't have any result, but the woman, anxious to have a colt, wouldn't leave the pumpkin. That annoyed the farmer who, in his anger, kicked the pumpkin which fell in pieces and shook the pile of branches, from which a fine little white hare ran out.

The old woman, believing that it was the colt running away, began to run and to cry:

>   Oh! oh! alas, alack!
>   Oh! oh! alas, alack!

Not being able to catch it, she returned, very disappointed, to her old man, saying to him: "You see, if we'd waited some days longer we'd have had a fine little colt."

13   The Cobbler

Once there was a cobbler and his wife. The cobbler wanted to eat pancakes one morning. That made his wife say to him: "We have no frying pan. I'm going to borrow one from the neighbour." He went to fetch the flour and she went to fetch the frying pan. Then she mixed the pancakes. He ate the pancakes as usual. Then the wife said: "Now you're going to return the frying pan."

"No, it isn't me, it's you who's going to return the pan."

"No, I'm not going to return it. You go to return it."

"No, I'm not going there at all."

Then they made a pact that the one who spoke the first word would return the pan. The fact was that he was a cobbler. He stitched with his wax thread and sang:

> De ri de ri de ri de rum dum dum dou dou!
> De ri de ri de ri de rum dum dum dou dou!

She also had her little song:

> Tadl-la dl-la dl-la dl-la da da da da!
> Tadl-la dl-la dl-la dl-la da da da da!

There came a knock at the door. They both went on singing without stopping. There were three or four knocks at the door. Then when there was no reply someone pushed the door and came in. The traveller asked what road to take to get to the fifth line. They still sang, they sang, they sang the same little songs.

The traveller was annoyed. He said to the cobbler: "If you don't speak to me I'm going to squeeze your wife in the corner." The wife went over and sat in the corner. The traveller approached the wife. She let him squeeze her in the corner.

The cobbler watched astounded. He didn't want to speak but at last he cried, "Let her go."

His wife said: "You return the pan! It's you who has spoken the first word!" She went in the corner on purpose to make him speak.

14   The Lousy-Head

Once there was a man and his wife and they were both stubborn. His wife, she had made some soup. She said to her husband, she said, "It's good soup, yes?" (I forgot to tell you that they were newly married.) This is what she said: "I've made good soup, my husband?"

He said, "It is salty!"

"Yes, it's good, isn't it?"

"Yes indeed, it is salty!"

"Yes, indeed, it is good, isn't it?"

"Yes, it is good, but it is salty!"

"Yes indeed, in any case it is good? Say that it is good!"

"It is salty!"

Then she said, "You are a lousy-head!"

He said, "Don't say that! I'm going to drown you."

"Yes indeed, you are a lousy-head!"

"Very well, I'm going to drown you!"

"Do what you will, but you are a lousy-head!"

Then he took his wife and threw her in the water; then she sank in the water. She kept saying: "You are a lousy-head!"

"Take it back because I'm going to drown you!"

"You are a lousy-head!"

Then it covered the woman right under her arms. "You are a lousy-head!"

It came up to her neck. "You are a lousy-head!"

When her head had been covered by the river, well she raised her arms in the air pretending to kill lice to show that he was still a lousy-head.

15   The Two Neighbours

There were once two neighbours. One was a rich sheep-dealer and people whispered rather strange comments about his way of making deals. The other was a poor beggar who had arrived in the village a little while earlier. People also talked about him for, since his arrival, several thefts had been committed. Some even claimed to have seen the beggar arrive at his home in the early morning with full bundles on his back.

One day a man appeared at the rich trader's house and said that he wanted to buy some sheep. The trader quickly led the buyer to his sheep pen and some time later the stranger left carrying a sheep on his back. He had no sooner left the place than the seller hurried to the beggar's house and said, "I've just sold a fine sheep, the best in my sheep pen. The man is leaving with the sheep on his back. I thought that you could relieve him of his burden for he has a long way to travel. If you succeed, we'll share as before." "That's understood," replied the beggar. "I'm going right away."

The beggar dressed and took along a fine pair of new shoes that he'd got last evening, although how he got them no one knew. He cut across the fields as the road that the buyer had taken made him cross a large forest. The beggar arrived first. He put one of the shoes at the entrance to the wood and went to put the other fifteen arpents further on; then he crouched in the bushes near by and waited. Soon the man with the sheep on his back came. He saw the shoe, stopped, and said, "A fine shoe, it's a pity there isn't a pair," and he went on his way.

Fifteen arpents later, seeing the other shoe, he put his sheep on the ground and retraced his steps to look for the first one. When he returned his sheep had disappeared. The beggar had carried it away.

The next day the same man appeared again at the trader's house and said, "I had a misfortune yesterday, I lost my sheep, and I've come to see if you'll sell me another."

"Certainly," the trader replied. "Come choose one." He sold him the same sheep without the buyer realizing it. As soon as he left, the trader went again to find his neighbour, the beggar, and proposed again to share the proceeds if he'd kidnap the sheep. "Agreed." The beggar went out this time with some chunks of salty bacon which he scattered along the path to the forest. Then he hid in the bushes as he'd done the first time, waiting. The buyer came soon, saw the little chunks of salty bacon, but didn't pay much attention at first. Then seeing the bacon chunks multiply, he put his sheep on the ground to return to collect them. When he came back he realized that his second sheep had disappeared.

The next noon the rich trader saw his buyer arrive and hastened to sell him yet another sheep, the same one he'd sold twice before. As soon as he'd left, the merchant went to the beggar's house and made him the same proposal. The beggar thief this time took nothing with him. He hid himself in the forest a little distance from the road and waited for the man who wasn't long in appearing. Immediately the beggar started to imitate the sheep's cry. "Baa-a-a Baa-a." The man stopped and listened. "Well, well, I think I'm going to recover my sheep." He put his sheep on the ground and plunged into the forest, running. The beggar imitated the sheep's cry so well that he led the man astray, doubled back, and arrived at the road. He seized the sheep and fled. When the buyer came back he found that his third sheep had disappeared. Did he ever realize that he'd been tricked? The fact remains that he also disappeared. He didn't return to the rich trader's home and they never saw him in the village.

As for the two neighbours, when the time for sharing the profits came the rich trader gave the beggar only a third of the money. The latter said nothing but after three days the merchant noticed that he was missing three sheep. He suspected the beggar. He got ready to visit him but while dressing he found that the money he'd made from selling the sheep had also disappeared.

He ran to his neighbour's house. The beggar had gone, but he'd taken great care to nail over his door a notice bearing these words:

Thieves, whether poor or rich,
Are both friends of the devil.
The one who plays his trick last
Is the one who laughs best.

16   The Calf Sold Three Times

There was a poor devil of a habitant who ended by drinking all his wealth. He had left only a young spring calf. He goes out then to sell it, in order to have some money to drink.

On the way he meets the village doctor whom he knew well. He stops him and says: "Well, friend, won't you buy a fine calf this morning?" "How much?" "A sovereign." "Done." And the doctor pays for the calf and tells the habitant to bring him to his house for he was called to a patient and couldn't take him home at the moment.

The habitant continues on his way and soon meets the notary. "Well, friend, won't you buy a fine calf this morning?" "How much?" "A sovereign." "Done." And, like the doctor, the notary pays and tells the habitant to lead the calf to his place for he was called to an invalid's home to draw up a will.

Some distance before reaching the village the habitant meets the lawyer and says to him: "Well, friend, won't you buy a fine calf this morning?" "How much?" "A sovereign." "Done. Take him to my home for I have to go to the next village on pressing business."

The habitant goes then to the village, stops at a tavern, spends his silver, then climbs into his wagon, taking his calf home with him.

The doctor, the notary, and the lawyer were very surprised on returning to find that the habitant hadn't delivered the calf bought that morning. They spoke together and finally decided to arrest the dishonest habitant. The habitant goes to find a lawyer in a neighbouring place and confides his case to him. The lawyer, listening to the account of the case, says: "Your case, sir, is very difficult to defend. Your dishonest act is too clear. However, there's one way of winning this case. Each time that the judge or prosecutor asks you a question, you reply only with these words: 'Oink, oink, oink!' "

And so when the time of the trial comes, the judge, addressing himself to the habitant, questions him thus: "Sir, have you sold a calf to the doctor here?" "Oink, oink, oink," replies the habitant. "Also to the notary?" "Oink, oink, oink." "Is it the same calf that you sold to the lawyer?" "Oink, oink, oink." "But you haven't delivered your merchandise to these gentlemen."

"Oink, oink, oink." "Why haven't you delivered what you sold?" "Oink, oink, oink." After several questions, the judge, receiving no other reply, says: "You see, sirs, that this man is crazy. I order that he be let go in peace."

The lawyer engaged to defend the habitant goes to find him and says joyfully: "Now that I've won your case, You're going to pay me for my work." "Oink, oink, oink," was the reply that he received. "See here, it's ten dollars, you're not going to be begged to pay me. "Oink, oink, oink." "See here, you can't put on that lunacy with me. It's I who have won for you." "Oink, oink, oink." "See here, must I get angry to make you pay?" "Oink, oink, oink." And the defender, no more than the doctor, the notary, and the lawyer, got no other satisfaction.

Which proves that in this little case as in many others, the lawyer and the habitant had learned nothing about honesty.

17 Richard's Cards

One day a man named Richard is passing a church and goes in to hear the holy Mass.

Richard goes to a pew by the wall where you hear and see the best. There, instead of taking a book of devotions from his pocket, he drew out a deck of cards. The constable's finger motions him to leave the church. But Richard does not move. The constable goes to him and says, "Instead of amusing yourself with a deck of cards, take a book of devotions." Richard replies, "After Mass I'll explain my deck of cards to you."

The Mass over, the priest and the constable come to reproach Richard, who replies: "If you'll let me, I'll explain my deck of cards."

"Speak, Richard," replied the priest, "I'll let you."

Richard draws the deuce and says: "The deuce represents to me the two Testaments."

Drawing the trey: "The trey reminds me of the three persons of the Holy Trinity; the four represents the four evangelists; the five, the five books of Moses; the six represents the six days that God took to create heaven and earth; and the seven, the day when He rested, after the creation."

Drawing the eight, he said, "The eight reminds me of the eight people saved from the Flood."

Drawing the nine . . . [the nine ungrateful lepers].

Drawing the ten: "The ten represents God's Ten Commandments."

Drawing the Queen: "She reminds me of the Queen of Heaven."

Drawing the King: "The King represents the only Master to Whom I owe obedience."

Drawing the ace: "The one and same God Whom I adore."

The priest says, "Richard, I notice that you've missed the Jack."

"Father, if you'll let me speak, I'll satisfy you."

"Speak, Richard, I'll let you."

"Father, the Jack represents to me a real rascal, just like your constable here."

18   The Dreams of the Hunters

I'd like to tell you that once there were three gentlemen and their cook who went hunting in the woods. After hunting all day without eating, they had killed only one partridge. They said: "Let's keep this partridge for breakfast. It will be for the one who has the finest dream."

The next morning: "What did you dream?" they asked each other. One of them replied: "Me, I dreamed that I was married to the most beautiful princess in the world." The others said: "Ah, you had a fine dream." "Me," said another, "I dreamed of the Holy Virgin, that I saw her in all her beauty." The third: "Me, I dreamed that I was in heaven, where I saw the good God himself."

The cook added: "Me, also, I had a fine one. I dreamed that I had eaten the partridge, and I see that my dream is true because I can't find it this morning."

IV   Formula Tales

Most stories are interesting because of their characters or plots, but, in a small group of tales the form is more important than either characters or plot. These are the formula tales which include cumulative, endless, circular, unfinished, and catch tales. Stith Thompson notes that: "The effect of a formulistic story is always essentially playful, and the proper narrating of one of these tales takes on all the aspects of a game."

"The Little Mouse and the Little Fire-Coal" follows the familiar pattern of the cumulative tale, best known in English Canada through the nursery rhymes "The House That Jack Built" and "The Old Woman and Her Pig." It is also typical of many stories told to children where not only animals but objects are personalized. A twelve-year-old girl told this version which she had heard from her grandmother.

"Jean Baribeau" is a good example of the endless tale that is circular: it comes to a certain point and then begins over again, the repetition continuing until the audience protests. This pattern is more common in songs than in tales: "The Bear Went over the Mountain" is a familiar example. The most common form of the circular tale runs something like this: "It was a dark and stormy night and the captain said to the mate, 'Tell us a story.' The mate began, 'It was a dark and stormy night and the captain said to the mate. . . . "

The French-Canadian form is more ingenious than most, incorporating more details and a second circular pattern.

The "Three Annoying Tales" illustrate three different formulas. The first is a kind of catch tale, resembling ones in which the teller frightens the listeners by yelling boo or jumping at them at an exciting part. The second is a typical "unfinished tale" in which the narrator quits just when interest is aroused. Some English songs and rhymes use a similar device: "If you want any more you can sing it yourself," or "If the bowl had been stronger my tale had been longer." Finally, the last is a typical "Endless Tale" which is so arranged that it can continue indefinitely. The two most common forms describe hundreds of sheep to be carried over a stream one at a time, or, as here, corn to be carried away a grain at a time.

19   The Little Mouse and The Little Fire-Coal

Once upon a time there was a little mouse and a little fire-coal. One day the little mouse said to the little fire-coal, "Do you want to cross the river?"

"How can you cross the river? We have no boat."

"That doesn't matter, we're going to put two strands of straw crosswise and we'll go over."

"You aren't crazy. You know that I would set fire to the straw and I'd drown."

"It's you who's crazy, little fire-coal. How can you set fire to the straw in the water? The water would put it out at once. Come on then, cowardy."

He protested a bit more but she teased him so much that he let himself be persuaded.

The little mouse took two strands of straw, put them cross-wise, and placed them on the river. She made the poor little fire-coal embark, although he was very scared. She pushed the straw into the open water. "Bon Voyage!" she cried. "I'll follow you soon."

Scarcely had she said that when she saw a little smoke on the water. The little fire-coal had set the straw on fire. He wanted to struggle but he fell in the water and died in spite of his efforts. The little mouse who saw him drowning laughed like a little fool. She laughed so hard that she split her little belly. "Well," said she, "that serves me right. I'm punished for what I did. Now what to do? I'll go to the cobbler to stitch me up."

And away she goes. She walks and walks. With pain and misery she reached the cobbler's.

"Good cobbler, will you please stitch my little belly?" "I'd mend you gladly but I haven't any hair to make my wax thread. Go ask the sow to give me some hair to make my wax thread, and I'll stitch your little belly."

She goes on . . . reached the sow's pen. "Good sow, will you give me some hair for the cobbler to make his wax thread and stitch my little belly?" "I'd give them to you gladly but I have nothing to eat. Go tell the miller to send me some bran and I'll give you some hair for the cobbler."

She goes to the miller's house. "Good miller, will you give me some bran for the sow who will give me some hair for the cobbler to mend my little belly?" "I'd give it to you gladly but I haven't any grain to grind. Go ask the field to give me some grain and I'll give you some bran."

Poor little mouse, there she goes. She walks and walks, holding her guts in her hands. She reaches the field. "Good field, will you give me some grain for the miller so that he will give me some bran for the sow who will give me some hair for the cobbler so he can mend my little belly?" "Why do you want me to give you some grain? I'm quite poor. Go tell the ox to give me some manure to fertilize me and I'll give you some grain for the miller who'll give you some bran for the sow who'll give you some hair for the cobbler so he can mend your little belly."

She goes on then to find the ox who gives her some manure which she carries to the field which gives her some grain for the miller. The miller gives her some bran which she carries to the sow. The sow gives her some hair for the cobbler. The cobbler uses the hair for his wax thread and then stitches the mouse's little belly. The little mouse thanks the cobbler and goes away running, promising no more to rip her little belly.

Me, I stepped on the tail of the little mouse who said "Squeak! squeak!" My story is ended.

20 Jean Baribeau

Jean Baribeau was born to poor parents who were thieves. They who loved him with a most tender love drove him away from their house at the age of three. Then he headed toward the capital to complete his studies.

But the political struggles and the sorrows of love led him soon to the gates of the tomb. They called in the most renowned doctors, and again thanks to their enlightened care he died. His fiancée erected a magnificent monument on which these words were carved: "Here lies Jean Baribeau, born of poor parents who were thieves. They loved him with the most tender love. . . . ." (*Begin again and repeat at will.*)

(*After some recriminations from the listeners that this repetition is boring, the story-teller pretends to leave the vicious circle in which he turns, and changes the story thus:*)

His fiancée gave him the most magnificent funeral. Everyone wept; the chief of the firemen wept into his helmet. When his helmet was already full, a tear slid, fell, germinated, sprouted. The king's son, passing by, tripped, fell, killed himself. His father, who loved him to distraction, gave him a magnificent funeral. Everyone wept; the chief of the firemen wept . . . . (*Begin again.*)

(*After having thus made fun of his listeners twice, the story-teller can usually enjoy a well-earned rest.*)

21   A Catch Tale

There was once a little boy who wanted to go bathing. His father forbade him: "Take heed not to go bathing for if you happen to drown I will give you a good spanking."

The little boy went out secretly and, unfortunately, he drowned himself. When they brought the body to the house, his father moved forward saying: "Ah, you disobeyed us, you have been bathing and you have drowned. Look, you are going to get a good slap as I promised you."

(*Here the story teller starts to smack the children who are listening to the story and they don't like it when he tells this story often!*)

22   An Unfinished Tale

Once there was an old old man and an old old woman who lived on a high mountain. They had lived there a long time. And if they haven't gone, they live there still.

(The storyteller pretends to pay attention to something and stops. The children are there waiting for the rest which doesn't come. If they protest, the storyteller begins the same thing again.)

23 An Endless Tale

One year the harvest was very good. A farmer had filled his barn with oats. It was a good barn, but in the wainscotting there was a board with a little hole. Now this year, suddenly, there came down in the parish swarms of grasshoppers who destroyed everything they could reach. Having laid waste everything outside, they came to besiege the barn filled with oats. As the hole in the board was small, it allowed only one grasshopper through at a time.

(*Then the storyteller begins the refrain that follows:*)

One grasshopper enters, takes out a grain; one grasshopper enters, takes out a grain; one grasshopper enters, takes out a grain . . .

(*He continues until the children cry and protest. Then the storyteller makes a small diversion by beginning again:*)

The barn was filled with oats, but there were a great many grasshoppers. As the hole in the board was small, only one grasshopper entered at a time. One grasshopper enters, takes out a grain . . . (*and thus he continues indefinitely.*)

V   Legends

Where the "contes populaires" are recognized as fictional and use ancient plots known in many countries, the "légendes" or "anecdotes populaires" are told as true stories and are more closely linked to a particular area. Although many of them have counterparts in other countries, they are usually given a specific French-Canadian locale and hence they reflect more closely the beliefs, traditions, and customs of the rural French Canadians. They deal with such subjects as hidden treasure, lutins (goblins), feux-follets (will-o'-the-wisps), the chasse-galerie (flying canoe), loups-garous (werewolves), sorcerers, and encounters with the devil. Most of them use widespread motifs, but they are all nicely localized and told as true.

Perhaps the most popular of all the French-Canadian legends is the one variously titled "Rose Latulippe," "Le Diable à la dance," or "Le Diable, beau danseur." Dr. J.-E.-A. Cloutier of Cap-Saint-Ignace, Montmagny, heard the version following from several people in L'Islet, but mostly from the octogenarian widow of Joseph Caron. This version is more detailed than most and shows clearly the influence of religion on the local legends. It gives a good picture of social gatherings in rural Quebec and includes many words and phrases from the local idiom.

This famous tale first appeared in print in 1837 when Philippe Aubert de Gaspé, fils, published L'Influence d'un livre. He called the tale simply "L'Étranger"—The Stranger—and attributed it to an old farmer of the Montreal region. He named the girl with whom the Devil danced Rose Latulippe and had her entering a convent, and he did not have the Devil revealed by a child. The fact that such details differ from the oral tales is evidence that de Gaspé's version was not the original from which the oral versions sprang. The tale was well known all along the lower St. Lawrence with minor variations and usually with local details like the reference to the hole through which the Devil fled in Dr. Cloutier's version. One informant, Eleonore Turgeon, even claimed to have known the heroine, a Miss Bolduc, of Saint-Isadore, Dorchester.

Another legend almost equally popular and widespread in French Canada tells how the Devil in the form of a horse is forced to haul materials for building a church. Again our version comes from Dr. Cloutier who sent it to Dr. Barbeau in 1919, retelling it as he had heard it from Angèle Boulet at L'Islet some thirty years earlier. There are versions of this tale locating the church that the devil built in at least nine different villages in Quebec.

"The Black Dog at Le Rocher-Malin," about an encounter with the Devil in the form of a dog, illustrates the firm belief characteristic of legends, with the narrator assuring us that he heard it from the very woman involved. In introducing it, Dr. Barbeau noted that Le Rocher-Malin (literally, Wicked Rock) of Notre-Dame-du-Portage, Témiscouata, is a famous haunted place. Instead of ghosts, it was the Devil, known locally as Charlot, who made it feared. The Devil was reputed to disguise himself as a big dog with human speech, as in this tale; or in other tales as a small dog that incessantly pursued travellers, or a giant who took a wicked pleasure in harassing those who travelled along the highway at night.

Unlike the first three stories which are local Quebec legends, "The Bee and the Toad" and "The Winter of the Crows" are examples of the international religious legends which have been termed "the Bible of the folk." They naturally took root in Quebec, reflecting the long dominance of the Catholic religion. Most Biblical legends deal with the Creation or the Flood, and the story of how God made the bee and the Devil made the toad is typical of the creation legends, while "The Winter of the Crows" deals with the other major theme, the flood. Both also illustrate a very prominent feature in legends: their use to explain how birds or animals acquired their particular characteristics. The tale of how ravens acquired their black colour and their harsh voices is very widespread but the storyteller has given it a Canadian slant by having the ill-fated birds spend their exile in northern Canada—and the ending illustrates how adults sometimes used legends to admonish their children.

The French-Canadians tell many stories of encounters with various supernatural creatures. The loup-garou is the Canadian counterpart of the European werewolf (literally man-wolf)—a human being transformed into a wolf or able to assume wolf form. The superstition came to New France with the first settlers: the voyageurs believed in it, and it came to be confused with the Wendigo of the Algonkian Indians. The loup-garou is usually considered to be controlled by Satan and to have been transformed because of a curse or as a punishment for not going to mass or confession, usually over a period of seven years. He is reputed to eat human flesh, and to return to human form at daybreak.

"Feu-follet" is translated as "will-o'-the-wisp," but the English term does not have the same connotation. A feu-follet is a wicked spirit that wanders at night in the shape of a flame or ball of fire, usually around swampy spots, trying to lead humans astray. Many people claim to have seen them, and they offer different explanations of what they are. Charles Barbeau, who told of "The Feu-Follet and the Knife," explains them as spirits that God has sent to earth to do penance but who do evil instead. Others say they are persons who have sold themselves to the Devil, or ones the Devil has changed into feu-follets because they didn't go to confession for seven years. Still others conceive of them as similar to loups-garous: persons who change into feux-follets at night and revert to human form in the day. There is a belief you can defend yourself against one by sticking a needle or a knife in a tree; the feu-follet then must wear himself out trying to pass through the eye of the needle, giving the traveller time to reach home safely.

The lutins are little mythical creatures abounding especially in Celtic tradition and corresponding roughly to goblins, elves, or fairies. There are various categories: lutins of the air, the night, the forests, the mountains, the rivers, and the stables, and it is the lutins of the stables that seem to predominate in Canada. Most of the stories tell of them braiding horses' manes or tails to make stirrups, and riding them at night across the fields, leaving them at daybreak white with foam. A widespread belief holds that lutins have to leave everything in its place as they found it, so to get rid of them, a farmer would spill a little bran at the stable door; then when the lutins scattered the bran, they had to return all the tiny particles to their place. Dr. Barbeau said that the storytellers believe in them so firmly that they claim to have seen their horses' manes braided some hundreds or even thousands of times.

Beliefs in forerunners or death warnings are also very widespread. These take many forms: a bird in the house, or a dog howling are among the most common, but a great variety of things have been considered death warnings. In "The Three Drops of Blood" the blood and the ghost wailing combine two dramatic signs, although in this story they are not so much forerunners as messages telling of a death taking place at a distance.

In introducing a group of tales about witchcraft, Dr. Barbeau noted that for a long time witches and wizards in Canada as well as in France enjoyed a prestige that the clerics did not succeed in dispelling. He identified the two magicians of "The Wizard's White Magic" as Pierrot Dulac and the "Grand Jacquot" who lived in Saint-François, Beauce, where they enjoyed a certain notoriety for more than sixty years. Dulac was said to cast spells and counter-spells; he caused illnesses so that he could cure them. His rival, the Grand Jacquot, provoked a competition to establish which of the two was the greater wizard.

The last two are perhaps the most characteristic of all the French-Canadian legends. The death of Cadieux is the earliest and most widespread of the native French-Canadian tales, and his "complainte" is believed to be the first song composed in Canada about a Canadian incident. Cadieux is said to have died in 1709, and by 1800 his story was known to almost every voyageur. Many early travellers and fur-traders mention the legend, and at least thirteen different versions of the song have been collected.

Dr. Barbeau noted that George Nelson was the first to write of the story in his manuscript Journal of 1802 where he spoke of a canoe that had "a miraculous escape" and of "one unfortunate creature" who was found dead "in a hole he had himself dug out with a paddle." Then about 1820 John J. Bigsby heard the same tale incorporated in a song.

Apparently the story of Cadieux was based on a real incident, but it very early acquired such legendary details as the vision of the Virgin Mary that guided the canoe, and the verses written in blood on a sheet of birchbark. Joseph-Charles Taché gave one of the most complete accounts of the story and song in his Forestiers et voyageurs, first published as a book in 1884 and frequently reprinted.

The tale of the flying canoe is so popular and so widely known that "La Chasse-Galerie" has almost become a symbol for French-Canadian culture. It is of course merely a local version of the many tales of aerial hunts known throughout Europe. Dr. Barbeau noted that the term came from a legend about Seigneur Gallery of Poitou who was condemned to an eternal hunt, and that the form "galerie" is from a false Canadian etymology in which the word signified an elevated platform on the outside of a house.

Honoré Beaugrand published the first account of the tale in La Patrie (in 1891 and in other journals later; it was incorporated in a book), La Chasse-Galerie et autres legends in 1900 and reprinted in 1973. In his introduction to the new edition François Ricard said that a legendary story is a tale in which the supernatural is localized and the narrator identified with the protagonist. Hence the only way for a writer to publish the authentic legendary stories would be to relate them in the first person. He notes that "La Chasse-Galerie" and "Le Fântome de l'Avare" are the most successful pieces in Beaugrand's book because the inspiration and atmosphere of the legendary story are perfectly reproduced: "Everything happens as if the writer did not exist, or, better, as if his task had been only to register, to reproduce the word of the old cook who ran the chasse-galerie." In his own introductory note Beaugrand wrote that "the story is based on a popular belief from the time of the coureurs de bois and voyageurs of the northwest. The shantyboys continued the tradition and it is essentially in the river parishes of the St. Lawrence that the legends of the chasse-galerie are known. I have met more than one old voyageur who claimed to have seen the bark canoes travel in the air filled with the possessed, going to see their sweethearts, under the sponsorship of Beelzebub."

24   The Devil at the Dance

They were very good people in the home of François C . . . , not proud, religious, charitable to the poor, not haughty. They owned little. Besides, they were straight as the king's sword. And when they were selling, they gave generous measure, always a good trait. They never spoke ill of anyone; and they never missed the First Friday of the month. Why, to tell all, they were first-class people.

It isn't often that they had a dance in this house. But the reason, this year, was that young François, their son, had just returned from a great trip to a distant country with Captain Basile Droy. They had to have a feast for his arrival.

Always at François C . . . 's home there'd be a great party the day after Twelfth Night. After supper a great many guests came, a lot of young people especially. They followed the great Dédé from the top of the island who was a fine fiddler and singer. It disturbed Mother Catherine when she saw many come who weren't invited, but she was too good-natured to make a fuss. After all, they were all childhood friends of young François.

Toward nine o'clock the great musician took out his fiddle from its fine varnished case. He began to pass the rosin over the bow. Then zing, zing, he started to chord. Ho, then, some hymn tunes, some songs: "Nouvelle agréable," "Ça bergers," "En roulant ma boule." After that it was some simple jigs, and then reels. Why, one could never miss the chance to hear such fine music!

Young François, with Germain Chiasson, little Blanche's suitor, and José Moreau, who was nicknamed "Golden Throat" because of his fine talk, went to call his father into the study to speak to him in private. There he asked permission to dance some rigadoons. There's nothing wrong with that, is there? Father François had to be begged because of the priest's sermons, and also the unexpected guests, some of whom smelled of liquor. He went to consult his wife. Why, it was too bad to refuse this to young François who'd just returned from such a long voyage. So he gave permission.

As soon as he agreed, they cleared the middle of the room. Everyone settled around the kitchen. Old François opened the dance with his wife Catherine, in a simple jig with not a few flourishes, I'm telling you. Of fine steps there were many. I tell you that for old people of their age, it wasn't easy to match them. It was Pierre, his son, who came to relieve them with his wife, Manda Berton. They were two fine dancers also, but they didn't beat Father François and his wife, oh, no!

The great Dédé played like one possessed, tapping his heel, which there was nothing so fine to hear. He wasn't controllable, this lad, when he had a little shot. They organized reels, *casse-reels,* cotillions, *spendys,* *"salut-des-dames"* . . . The great Dédé seemed set for twenty-four hours. Between dances he stopped just long enough to take a little shot, then hurrying back, played all kinds of things—dances, songs, hymns, even laments. It went like real wildfire!

At eleven o'clock there was a little lull to catch breath. Suddenly they heard some small bells, then the sound of a sleigh which slid over the ice. *Crunch!* it said.

After a little while there's a knock on the door. "Come in," says Pierre. The door opens, then they see a tall handsome man with curly hair and a fine black beard cut to a point. He had lively black eyes which seemed to throw sparks. He had a fine beaver cloak, with a fine sealskin cape. He also had very fine moccasins of caribou, decorated with beads in thirty-six colours, and porcupine quills, also dyed all kinds of colours. He looked like a real gentleman indeed!

Then, just imagine! A fine sleigh gleaming like a mirror, with fine buffalo skins, a fine glossy black horse, with a white harness that had cost five or six gold coins. He looked unbelievably vigorous, this horse. He was all covered with hoar frost. All the horse dealers went around him to have a good look, but no one recognized him. He must have come from a distance. They offered to unharness him for the gentleman, but he refused, saying it wasn't worth the trouble, that he'd just put the fur robe on his back. He wouldn't be long. When passing he'd seen that people were enjoying themselves and he came in to dance a couple of dances.

They offered to take his wraps. He took off his cloak and cap but he wouldn't remove his kid gloves. The young people thought that was to show off, like city gentlemen, who did that, it seemed. At all events, I tell you that he certainly looked nice, that unexpected guest, and I assure you that the young women were strutting around and eyeing him. They wanted to know who would have the honour of dancing with this fine cavalier.

But as he was a great gentleman who knew how things were done, he went to ask the daughter of the house, Mamselle Blanche, who was not to be overlooked, you know. She was a fine-looking girl who had manners and a good bearing. She was a little shy at first; it took away some of her confidence. Imagine it, then, to dance with this gentleman before everyone, it was embarrassing. Also when he asked her like this: "Mademoiselle, will you do me the honour to dance with me?" she replied, blushing and trembling a little: "With pleasure, sir, but excuse me, I don't know how to dance very well." The little hypocrite, she knew very well that she was one of the best dancers on the island.

He wasn't only a beautifully dressed gentleman, this guest, my children; he was also a very fine dancer indeed, I assure you. Father François couldn't believe it and he was all dumbfounded: "My, my, what a fine dancer he is," he didn't tire of repeating to himself. He didn't know where he got all these steps. "He invents them, he invents them," he repeated endlessly.

The gentleman had begun by dancing a simple jig that lasted a good half hour. He seemed infallible. After little Blanche, all the best dancers at the party were rising in turn to face him, but he was coping with them all. He didn't seem tired as he came to make his first bow to his partner.

Several young men tried to replace him, but they lost the step quickly and he signed to them by waving with his arms to return to their place. After that he jigged two or three fine flourishes which were really something to see.

One would say that there was a game between the fiddler and him, to see which would outlast the other. Dédé was starting to feel weak, he was finding the game a little hard. He was sweating heavily. He was much too proud to slow up. He seemed rather to catch fire little by little, one would say that he was getting inspired. I'm telling you, the dust was flying under his feet, and he was tapping his heels always without losing a beat.

But suddenly *crack*, a broken string! Oh, the wretch, Dédé

had done it on purpose. Luckily, he had some spare strings. Meanwhile, while he restrung, it gave him time to catch his breath a little. The guest of honour took advantage of it to organize a spendy, with the participation of course of the handsome stranger who during that time was flirting with all the girls.

At last the fiddle was restrung. Dédé, replenished with a good shot of rum, seemed as fresh as at the beginning of the party.

"Gentlemen, pray take your place for a spendy," cried José Moreau in his fine singing voice, and they form up with more enthusiasm than ever. All this commotion finally ended by waking Pierre's little boy who was two years old. As Manda, who was doing the honours of the house, was too busy to take care of him, Grandmother Catherine had taken him on her knee, and then to amuse him she sat with him right in the door of the bedroom where the little one could enjoy the whirling of the dancers.

But each time the fine strange dancer passed before the child, he uttered cries of fright, and, gripping the old woman around the neck, he cried: "Bur . . . bur . . . burning, sir, burn . . . burning!" "I say, how strange he is this evening," Catherine said to herself. As these fits were repeated each time the dancer passed before the child, the old woman began to find this funny; then, suddenly she noticed that the stranger's black eyes pierced the child with looks full of hatred.

He was dancing at this time with a young girl who wore a fine golden cross on her neck. As he passed below her, Grandmother Catherine heard him ask the girl if she would exchange this cross for a fine locket decorated with diamonds and containing his portrait. She rose, ran into the bedroom where a small jug of holy water stood at the head of the bed. She dipped her trembling old fingers in it and, still holding the child in her arms, she came through the door, making a sign of the cross over the dancer. It was magical and frightening.

The Devil—for it was he in person—leaped to the ceiling, uttering a hellish cry. He wanted to spring toward the door but he saw over it a temperance cross mounted on a holly bough. Mad with rage, Satan threw himself through the stone wall, leaving behind him a great hole in the dark stone. Then they heard a fearful uproar outside. The Devil and his horse disappeared into the night; a trail of flames flashed under the horse's feet.

Everyone came out appalled, and saw that the ice was completely melted where the infernal horse had touched. It hardly needs saying that the party broke up then.

Next day a bricklayer came to fill up the hole where the Devil had passed, but he never succeeded. Each stone that he tried to put in seemed possessed by an unknown force, and nothing would make it stay in place. They had the house blessed again, but the opening still remains, as if God wished to give a continual warning.

The old stone house stands today. Facing the hole in the room there is always a chest of drawers where they set holy candles, and outside the wall you see all year round a cord of stove wood piled.

But since then they never dance in the stone house of François C. . . .

25 The Devil Builds a Church

You know, my children, there wasn't always a church at L'Islet. A long time ago when my great grandfather lived at L'Islet, there was only the curé at the Cap (Saint-Ignace). Then, to celebrate Easter, to get married, or to get the babies baptised, they had to go to the church at the Cap. As you can see, that was very inconvenient; it wasn't easy to go then, with the dreadful roads they had. Truly, they were just terrible. That's all there's to it!

But in justification, there weren't many people in the parish: a house here and there, two or three at the top, the Chiassons and the Cenrés, then Bénoni Cloutier, at the foot of the slope, whose wife was said to have brought him half a bushel of French piastres as a dowry—enough to make many hundred louis! There were also some fine buildings on the outskirts: first, the house of Seigneur Casgrain; then, of Aimable Bélanger, one of the biggest habitants of the parish; then, in the back, toward Trois Sammons, there were the Carons and Bouchers—that's all.

Aside from that, there were poor people who began to plough the land and who lived in little log houses. It was open, as you might say, to the edge of the water; the village of "Belles-amours" was only beginning to grow. Believe me, there was plenty of poverty in those days; they had to work hard. You don't know what it was like, you others, to take land covered with trees and clear it for the plough. You had to pull up the stumps and then gather up the rocks!

The curé from the Cap came every two weeks to say mass in a little wooden chapel just where the little funeral chapel stands today. Then one fine day the news came that the residents of L'Islet were going to have their own curé. I don't need to tell you that this brought great joy to everyone.

But mon Dieu, that poor curé who was coming to take charge of the parish had nothing. No church, no parsonage, he had at first to live at the seigneur's house. Then they built him a kind of parsonage, something very wretched, where the poorest today would hardly stay. But monsieur le curé was quite content. He wasn't at all proud, this good M. Panet. All the priests are very good, my children, but this one was a saint, a true saint.

They say that he always went to carry the Host bareheaded, even in the worst cold of winter.

Sometime after his arrival it was decided to build the church. But monsieur le curé was indeed at a loss to know how to get the stone hauled for this building. Horses were scarce in the parish, and there were scarcely enough to do the work. There was no off-season.

Then one night, as he sat up thinking how to go about it, all of a sudden he heard a voice calling him by name. "I'm hearing things," he thought. It called him a second time. Then he felt alarmed, but said to himself, "I'm in a state of grace; I have nothing to fear." And he replied, "Whoever you are, in the name of God, what do you want of me?"

A beautiful lady in white appeared to him. "Have no fear, François," she said. "I am Nôtre Dame du Bon Secours; trust me and go to sleep. Tomorrow morning when you wake, you'll find a horse tied at the door of your house. Use him to haul stone for your church; you can make him draw heavy loads; he is very strong. But you must take one precaution: never remove his bridle. His bridle is blessed and if anyone takes it off him he'll disappear forever." The apparition vanished; then M. Panet fell asleep in his chair.

That was in the month of May, 1768. At half past four the sun shone into the curé's chamber and he awakened and started up. He immediately remembered his vision of the previous night but he believed he had been dreaming. He was kneeling to pray when suddenly he heard a horse pawing the ground outside. He looked out into his garden. What was his surprise to see a magnificent black horse tied to a tamarack!

He passed his hand over his eyes two or three times to make sure he was awake. Then he went out to convince himself over and over that he wasn't dreaming. It was indeed true, the vision that he'd had during the night. He put his hand on the horse's neck to assure himself once more that he wasn't deceiving himself. The horse trembled but didn't move a foot.

At five o'clock the workmen began to arrive for their day's work. "My friends," said the curé, showing them the horse, "someone has loaned me this beast to draw the stone for the church. It seems to be a good horse but it's a little difficult; be careful; above all, never take off his bridle, not even to let him eat or drink or for anything, because he'll escape from you."

"What do you call your horse, monsieur le curé?" asked Germain-à-Fabien Caron.

"Yes, let's see," said the curé. Then after some moments' reflection he said, "He's called Charlot. I place him in your charge."

"Well, I'll see to it, monsieur le curé. All the same, it's a funny name for a horse, Charlot. But it doesn't matter; if he isn't stubborn he'll do fine."

"For that," said the curé smiling, "I'll guarantee him."

They harnessed Charlot to a little cart with low wheels used for hauling rocks. They put on him first a reasonable load but Charlot went with it as if it was empty. The curé who saw them come said not to hesitate to load him more heavily. They loaded, then they loaded more, but it never seemed to tire Charlot. They made another cart twice the size, then they loaded it like a load of hay. The wheels cracked, but Charlot still went straight ahead.

What a horse that Charlot was, my children! Black as a crow, not a white hair, four good feet, and such legs! With it a superb rear; a fine free-wheeling neck. And how he carried his tail, my friends! Ah, he was a remarkably fine horse. A fine-looking horse indeed, but he had a wicked mouth. Monsieur le curé had warned them to be careful to keep away from his mouth. But since no one had to bridle or unbridle him it didn't matter. From time to time monsieur le curé, who was always with the workmen when he wasn't visiting the sick or hearing confessions, asked Germain, "Well, my Germain, how do you find him, your Charlot?" "Number one, monsieur le curé."

It had always been he who drove him. But this day he couldn't come, he was going to get his child baptized. And it was Rigaud-à-Batisse Bernier who replaced him. Rigaud was a good fellow and a great worker, but stubborn and conceited, thinking himself cleverer than everyone else. He was quite boastful as well, without equal. To hear it, there was nothing to compare with what he had.

His horse lacked nothing except speech; his cow was a real fountain; its milk was all cream; his pigs grew fat simply from the heat of the sun; his dog was smarter than many people; his hens laid two eggs a day; his land was so rich that it needed to be held in check; his wife made the best pancakes; his daughter had refused a Quebec lawyer who was coming all the time but who never appeared.

Besides he was a horseman such as one seldom sees. He was half a horse, see. He loved the horses that were very fast. For a long time he kept looking at Charlot, criticizing Germain-à-Fabien behind his back. Also, when he had this fine horse on his hands, he could hardly keep from laughing. You could say that it suited him down to the ground. It was "my horse" here, "my Charlot" there. "Gee up, whoa." You could hear nothing but his chattering.

Germain had warned him against removing the bridle to let him drink. But Rigaud replied, "Don't fret, Germain, I know horses; it's not the first that I bridle, and if I wish to unbridle him, the Devil will carry me off if I'm not able to rebridle him."

So this day Rigaud was overjoyed. He was hauling stone from the other side of the Turtle River. It was the middle of August and very hot. Crossing the river, Rigaud, who was thirsty, stopped his horse in the middle of the stream. There he drank two or three good gulps from the hollow of his hand. After that he wanted to make his horse drink. He whistled two or three times but the horse seemed not to care.

Rigaud thought, "He's handicapped by his bridle. It isn't sensible not to unbridle a horse to let him drink. Who ever heard of that? The curés, what do they know about horses? Poor beast! I'm going to unbridle him for a little, I'm sure he's thirsty." He put his hand in his mane to make friends, he unbuckled the bit; gently, watching carefully, he raised the bridle . . . whoo . . . sssh! Charlot, in a flash, took off at full speed, dropping harness and cart into the river. Rigaud was thrown fifteen feet away and floundered in the water. Charlot ran off along the highway at an astonishing pace.

He reached the shore where the Monument stands today. M. Panet, head bare, had just come from taking the Host to an invalid when he caught sight of the escaping horse. Recognizing Charlot, he stood in the middle of the road and made the sign of the cross to stop him. The horse reared and, leaving the road, he raced right north to the cliff that overhangs the river at this spot. Then he made a frightful uproar; the rock split from top to bottom, making a crack five or six feet wide. Down it the Devil plunged into hell, making a deep crack in the rock. That is the

Devil's Cave. . . . . Why! Who in the parish doesn't know about the Devil's Cave? The cave, made as if by axe blows in the rock with two fathoms of earth, its black mouth turned from the bank, seems forever to defy the great north winds.

Children always look at it with curiosity and a certain residue of fear. The most mischievious ask themselves how he had the power to cut into the rock so deep, this great space like a little bedroom, which measures, I'm sure, a tall alder or two in height and two in width. Ah, yes, by bad luck it was indeed the work of the Devil. It's not a joke that the old ones have called it the Devil's Cave, or Hell's Gate.

M. Panet was indeed rather annoyed by Charlot's flight, not that he liked him very much (monsieur le curé knew indeed what fire burned in him, this horse, but he was doing so much work). But as the stone was nearly all piled on the spot it wasn't too serious. To tell the truth, this good curé wasn't intending to keep Charlot when he was finished with him. He was too honest and God-fearing for that.

Charlot, who was the Devil in horse's shape, as you've guessed, was insulted because they made him haul all the stone for the church against his will. It seemed that this was the tenth church that he had built. Why! it was as if he promised himself to get revenge by playing ugly tricks and casting spells on the inhabitants of L'Islet. That's why, before leaving, he wished to make a little retreat in the parish where he could practice his witchcraft at his ease, and where he could lie in wait to test his spells on passers-by when he had a chance.

For years and years not a Christian dared go in a carriage at night past the Devil's Cave without some accident happening to him. Sometimes it was a swingle-bar or even a rein that broke; sometimes it was a shaft or even a support that gave way; another time the horse reared and started to limp; or still another time the carriage stopped flatly, with a wheel blocked. There were horses which when taken there started to balk, since no horse ever wanted to pass. For many many years no horse would pass there without pricking up his ears and shaking as if he smelt something that frightened him and that nobody saw.

Some nights people heard moans or the rattling of chains. At other times they saw a black beast like a wolf with a horrible mouth breathing flames coming out of the cave.

A curious thing, it was only when monsieur le curé went to carry the Host that nothing happened. It was a sign that the Devil kept away from that, yes?

In the long run, it was not reassuring, and it was a nuisance. The young no longer dared to go to watch, nor to see their girls along there.

And all this was Rigaud's fault. Why, it's very clear, no? If he had listened to the curé, it wouldn't have happened like that. When monsieur le curé would have finished with Charlot, he'd have tied him to the tamarack, then he'd say to the Holy Virgin, "Come for him, your horse, I no longer need him; I thank you very much." Then Charlot would have been returned as he came. The Holy Virgin would have quickly sent him to his place, there's no denying that. He wouldn't come to disturb the people of L'Islet, I guarantee. That's what happened from not listening, my children.

All the curés did their best to stop these spells. They prayed, then they hung crosses and medals in the Devil's Cave, then holy branches, candles, and relics of the saints. They blessed the cliff on all sides. Nothing did any good. They said always, "The good Lord is stronger than the Devil. This is going to stop." But still it continued.

Then one evening when monsieur le curé Delâge had been praying to Nôtre Dame du Bon Secours, the patron of the parish, he saw the Holy Virgin in a dream and she told him, "If you wish to deliver your parishioners from the Devil's tricks, raise a cross near the rock."

No sooner said than done. The next day monsieur le curé set about accomplishing the wish of the Holy Virgin. He spoke to the leading men of the parish and everyone started to work.

They competed as to which would give the most work days and bring the finest materials: some would bring the best cut stone; others fine pine beams; others fine cedars well squared and very sound; others still lime for the mortar; others pegs and forged nails.

Soon on the rock, since called "Monument," this fine cross arose, and the piety of the faithful of L'Islet has always striven to maintain it.

Before dedicating this fine monument, the good M. Delâge wanted to make a great housecleaning in the parish. He decided to hold a grand retreat as advocated by the late Monseigneur Mailloux, whom they called "the great vicar." This monsigneur was, as it were, a bishop, and he was dressed with unequalled finery: a beautiful cassock with purple buttons, a collar and purple lapels, and a square cap too.

It isn't enough to say that he speaks well, this priest! Mon Dieu, how fine his sermons were! Sometimes they said that he couldn't manage to say all that he thought, such a gift of speech he had! He never hesitated at all; and all that he said was always well worded with good sense. I tell you that he wouldn't spare the drunkards and blasphemers.

Also they came from everywhere, on all sides, from the third, fourth, fifth, even from the sixth concession; for at this time there was no Saint-Cyrille nor Saint-Eugène; all these concessions belonged to our parish. They passed crowded carriages and carts, women, children, old men, old women, in short, people such as we'd never seen or known. They came from I know not where. All these came to the retreat. Half had no pew, they had to sit on the banisters and then filled up the aisles.

In the retreat, people from a distance went to confess. Then, in the morning at daybreak, crowded carriages went from all sides towards the church to worship. There were some money-lenders who hadn't been to confession for ten, twenty, even thirty years, some people who'd been loups-garous, my children, who were converted. Oh, it was indeed fine. It had been decided that the Monument would be blessed the day the retreat ended.

All along the road as they left the church to go to the rock of the cross, they raised beacons of maples and plane trees. Then all around the Monument they put pine trees, lilac bouquets, all sorts of flowers and tents of all colours that several captains had loaned for the ceremony. Then later, after the grand mass, everyone went in procession, singing hymns. Those at the head of the procession had already reached the Monument while the last ones were still at the church.

Then everyone settled around the Monument on the banks, on the rocks, on the road, and in the neighbouring fields. And Monseigneur Mailloux, the fine golden cope on his back, with monsieur le curé Delâge and the curé from the Cap, like deacon and deputy deacon, mounted the great stairway, accompanied by several priests and minor clergy.

Then all went around the cross with the great silver vessel of holy water, Monseigneur sprinkling the cross and then all the priests, from all sides; at the same time they said the prayers in Latin. Afterwards Monseigneur made the finest of all his sermons. Everyone wept, as you might say. At the end he made the men at the foot of the cross promise that they would no longer drink or swear. He blessed us all once more and with a solemn voice he intoned the *Te Deum* while the procession went back on the road to the church.

(*M. Cloutier adds: Since the cross protects these formerly feared places, the Devil no longer dares to go out of his lair. There, below this great silent mouth of the cavern, children go to play without fear.*)

26   The Black Dog at Le Rocher-Malin

Le Rocher-Malin (in Notre-Dame-du-Portage, Témiscouta) got its name from the tricks the Devil played. I heard one of the stories of these tricks told by the very people who knew what happened.

It was a woman who was married to Nöel Perrault. At that time there was no doctor in the country, but there were some skilful women, midwives who had a special gift for healing. One fine day a birth was expected at the home of one of Mme Perrault's brothers, named Perron. The time come, Perron, whose house was near Le Rocher-Malin, went to look for Mme Perrault, who was staying with M. Michaud. Arriving there, he says, "My wife needs you; come quickly."

They go in haste, together, down the bank. As soon as they pass the end of the road by the brook, a big black dog faces them. The man is frightened. It's terrible. The woman says, "You're afraid? Just brace yourself a little. It's a dog like any other."

"Ah," he says, "It isn't a dog like any other." The dog did everything it could to prevent them from walking. Perron had to kick it to the side of the road in order to go on.

Mme Perrault said: "Don't upset yourself by fighting with the dog." She takes him by the arm and she drags him. The dog is always under their feet but he doesn't bite them.

They had three or four arpents to go. Before arriving, the dog comes in front of Perron and puts his two paws on his shoulders; he couldn't go ahead. The woman was brave—me, I know it—she helped him. They succeeded in getting right to the house, but the dog doesn't take his paws from his shoulders. When they reach the door, in leaving the dog says, "Your wife is dead."

The goodwife Perrault says, "You lie; she isn't dead." The woman wasn't dead, but she was near death.

This story I give you as I heard it told. It is Mother Perrault herself who told it.

27　The Bee and the Toad

When God had made the earth, the sun, the moon, and the stars, he put streams and trees and fruits upon the earth. Then he put Adam and Eve to live among them like a king and queen. They had everything they needed to make them happy. Among the thousand and one lavish sweet things, the bee should not be forgotten, this fine little insect that makes so much wax and honey. After the fall of the wicked angels, Lucifer, the leader of the infernal band, did everything he could to imitate or spoil the works of the All-Powerful.

One day when Adam and Eve were eating honey and delighting in this delicious food, Satan became jealous and looked for a way to spoil this source of their happiness. Creeping into their garden, he hid in a clump of briars near a beehive, and started to make a creature that would destroy the honey-bee.

As the good God had made the bee, which is the symbol of valour, of industry, and even of respect for authority (since the bees show so much respectful deference to their queen), that was a reason for Satan to want to destroy it.

He took a little earth and rolled it in his hands for a long time. When he had shaped this mud, he blew upon it three times, and muttered strange words, looking toward the beehive. Then he threw his newly-made creature in that direction.

But Satan was still new to the art of creation. He forgot to put wings on his new destructive friend which passed through the air and brushed against the honey-laden bees. They quickly lit on the branch of a tree, and the creature fell to the ground. Satan had made the toad. On falling it lay for a moment as though dead, and then it began to stir a little, then to gasp, and at last it breathed again.

Some bees who had left the swarm flew around in the air near the giddy creature; others soon followed to have a look at this new enemy unknown until then. The toad, waking up hungry, with the destructive instinct for which he had been created, started to jump and even managed to snap up some of the honey-bees that were circling around him.

From that day to this, wherever there are beehives, if you pass one in the evening at dusk and look carefully, you are sure to find one or more toads hidden near its mouth. They cannot help snapping as the bees enter and leave the hive. They are still ugly creatures, the living image of the Devil who made them.

28   The Winter of the Crows

After the patriarch Noah, following God's orders, had worked a hundred years to build the ark, he took on board it representatives of all the animal species on the earth, and lived there himself with his family.

Torrential rains fell from the sky and inundated first the valleys and plains and then the hills and even the highest mountains. The creatures living outside the ark perished down to the last one, save the fishes, and the ark, raised by the swelling waters, floated on the waves.

Much later, after the waters had gone back into the oceans, the lakes, and the rivers, Noah wished to make sure that the surface of the earth was again habitable. He opened a window and let out a raven, which until then had been the bird favoured from creation with bright and magnificent feathers and whose voice filled the air with joyful warblings.

"Fly over the surface of the earth," Noah commanded the raven. "If you find there any green trees, bring me a branch."

The raven saw some bodies floating in the water and, satisfying his voracious appetite, set out to devour them. He forgot his master's order, and no longer returned to the ark which had run aground on a mountain. Noah then cursed the raven for its faithlessness; his curse blackened the feathers of that bird and changed its warblings into a hoarse and plaintive croak.

The second time Noah sent the dove to look for green trees. The first time she returned with her beak empty; the second, she brought a green branch which bore fruit. The patriarch blessed the sweet messenger who became white and pretty, and who since has never ceased to be the bird beloved by all.

The time of liberation had come. Noah opened doors and windows and let out the captive species who spread out on all sides. As soon as he saw the crow, relative of the raven, flying past, he stopped it and, swayed by resentment, said to it: "You and your cousin the raven are condemned to travel forever without respite. Your tastes will be voracious and bloody, and your voices will break out in lugubrious cries. At your approach the elements will rouse up and by their anger chase you from their presence."

The crow, pursued by all the winged folk, fled uttering

lamentable cries. It took refuge in a deserted spot, then wandered alone and abandoned. For nourishment it gulped down the flesh that remained on the dead bodies beached in the slime. It met one day its cousin the raven who, like it, nourished himself on carrion. The crow and the raven, knowing themselves forever banished from the presence of man, bound themselves in friendship in their misfortune, and driven by remorse went away far toward the north.

After a long and painful journey they perched to rest on a tree in the midst of a great forest of pine and fir trees where peace and silence reigned. This forest had been one of ours, in Canada, for a long time. The ground, covered by a mantle of snow, had not the customary gloom of their deserts. The rays of the sun had here and there pierced through this white mantle, making it spotted. Everything smiled on the fugitives, who believed themselves at last sheltered from the opprobrium of man and nature.

The illusion of the raven and the crow did not last long. Early the next day their awakening was painful. The north winds, stirring at their approach, blew up a storm, and the sky, filled with threatening clouds, made the snowflakes swirl. The cold, coming from the north, gnawed piercingly into the exiles. They resumed their flight in front of the protests of the forest which refused them asylum.

Every year since that time the crows emigrate toward Canada at the coming of spring, and the forest rises up against them because of the curse of Noah.

The old man who, one spring a long time ago, told this legend to Adélard Lambert, of Berthier, began by these words: "Today the weather is fine, but it won't last long. I've seen three crows; they passed on the wing, going south. They seemed pursued by an invisible phantom."

At this explanation his wife added: "By passing they announced the little winter. Poor crows! They are paying very dear for a folly that dates back so far that one has almost forgotten it. And to say that they are condemned to undergo this injury right to the end of time!"

The same evening she told at length the legend of the crows to the children who questioned her; and she saw, with satisfaction, in their eyes the impression that her tale made on her small audience. She finished with the words: "If God's anger falls like that on the simple birds who were cursed by Noah, how much more his punishments will weigh on the faithless man who disobeys his commandments and scorns his representatives."

29 The Loup-Garou of the Cemetery

The old man Alexis Vallée said that there was a man who worked all day. But in the morning he was always miserable when he started work. He was always half dead. One time the old man Alexis stopped to take him to work. He said, "I think I'll not go to work today. I'm not well."

His wife spoke up and said, "You're going to work, as long as you're able to gad around at night."

My dead grandfather Vallée spoke up and said, "What? He spends the night gadding? In the morning he always gets to work after the rest."

His wife said, "You understand, Mr. Vallée, that this fellow has been married for thirteen years and has never stayed one night with me."

Her husband said, "What is it to you when I go around with my friends in the evening? Walking with friends is entertaining. The others will have some enjoyment, and me, I'll be bored like a poor dog." The discussion didn't last long. The fellow dressed and went to work with the old man Alexis.

That was at the beginning of the week. The rest of the week passed the same. Sunday this man always went to mass. Grandfather Vallée said, "I passed his place returning from mass, I saw the door open, I went in to have a drink—or at least pretend to. The fellow was lying in bed, his wife was in the kitchen crying. The house was double-locked. Curiosity came over me . . . I know it well. I asked her 'Why are you crying?' "

"I'm afraid, sir. I saw something for a few instants that really upset me. I tried to fight my husband's boredom. I've always had a wicked suspicion, and now I'm convinced of what I thought. It's the truth, my husband runs in the form of a loup-garou."

"I couldn't believe it—on hearing this my hair stood on end. But I said, 'How is it that he runs in the form of a loup-garou?' "

"She signalled me not to speak too loudly. She came to me at the door and told me that she'd found some threads from the nightcap of the neighbour, of the wife of the second neighbour who was dead. In her husband's big teeth there were still bits from the ties of the nightcap. She recognized the ties as she had herself made the nightcap to put on her head [when she was dead]."

And there it was stated, it was avowed by his wife, that he runs in the form of the loup-garou and that there were several like him, that they went to the cemetery to dig up the dead and eat them. He didn't want to believe it. When he died there was a big black dog under his bed and all the time that the corpse was there the dog didn't go out of the house.

The father Alexis Vallée told that for the very truth.

30 The Feu-Follet and the Knife

In earlier times people believed in feux-follets. They believed that they were spirits that the good God sent on earth to do penance and then instead of doing penance they devoted themselves to doing evil.

Joseph Busque himself told that one day he crossed a forest. It was very dark. He met a feu-follet who started to cross in front of him and repeated this often, crossing before Busque's eyes to prevent him seeing clearly in order to lead him into some chasm where he would die.

There was a saying that when someone was attacked by a feu-follet, he should take a needle and stick it in a tree; then the feu-follet had to pass through the eye of the needle. Busque didn't have anthing except his pocket-knife; he took it out, opened it, and stuck it in a tree. Then he closed it almost completely. The feu-follet had to pass through. Busque, undisturbed, went on his way, and the feu-follet stayed there.

Just as Busque was going to enter his house, as he opened the door, the knife came to stick in the door beside his head. The feu-follet had pulled out the knife and thrown it like that.

That was the saying and the belief of the people, I suppose.

31 The Lutin and the Quail

Prime Bolduc came to our place one evening and he spoke with papa. He told how to stop a lutin from braiding the horses' manes, and how to catch them.

When a horse had his mane braided by a lutin, the best way was to take a bowl of ashes and put it on the threshold of the stable door. When the lutin came in, he spilt the ashes and was obliged to gather it speck by speck. He had to do this quickly before the owner came in again.

Prime was a cunning man and he was angry. He had no fear of the Devil. He said, "One day I pondered how to try to catch a lutin. I put my bowl of ashes on the stable door. I said, 'Listen, Marie, you're going to come and knock on the door. I'm going to go out with a sack to the wicket gate of the stable. If he flees through there I'll catch him.'" Prime believed that when one caught a lutin or a Devil in one state he couldn't change during the time that you held him.

Prime goes out with his sack and Marie with her stick. Prime goes to the back of the stable and holds his sack. Damnation! Marie knocks on the door and Prime opens the sack. Suddenly, bang, bang, bang, it rings in the stable; the horses get up, there is an uproar—the horses are frightened—she keeps knocking on the door. Suddenly Prime feels something enter his sack, and thinks it's the lutin he has. "Damn it! I have it."

They go out and go into the house. "Go and get George"— speaking of papa. But Prime is too sly; he doesn't wait for George; he looks in his sack; he feels strong enough to overcome the lutin. He opens the sack: a hen quail. "Damnation! Marie, it's a hen quail. I've lost it [the lutin]."

That's what he believed, dear sir!

32   The Three Drops of Blood

Something happened twenty-five years ago at the home of Jérôme Saint-Laurent who was our second closest neighbour. My first cousin—Jérôme—was an honest man, a trustworthy man. He and his family were in the States. He was sick and tired of his birthplace. His wife said to him, "You're going to go down to Sainte-Anne. Perhaps you'll get better there." Anyway he came down here. He nursed himself a little and he began to feel better. He stayed all alone in the house.

Mr. Lebouthiller kept a store in Saint-Anne. Jérôme Saint-Laurent often went to the store when he needed something. One time he went up to Sainte-Anne, to the store, to buy some things. It happened that the clerk wasn't there. Saint-Laurent went into the house, but only the hired girls were there; the girls were washing up. He asked where the clerk was. They said he'd come in a minute, to sit down.

He began to chat with the girls. He was sitting near a window. He happened to see big drops of blood falling on the panes of the window on the west side. A girl says, "Look what's falling on the window." He starts to look from the inside, but the drops of blood were falling on the outside. He says, "That seems to be blood that's falling on the window-pane." They both go out, he and the hired girl, to see. They realize that it really was drops of blood that were falling. Jérôme says to the girl, "That must be a warning. Someone must have died in my family in the States—my wife or my children."

After the clerk came he made some small purchases and went back with them. When he'd gone to bed that night he heard moaning in the attic. The lamenting wasn't very loud. Jérôme wasn't a fearful man. He got up, lighted the lamp, and went to look in the attic. The moaning seemed to come from the south corner. As he went into the attic the moaning changed places. The moans were on the north side. He looked in the corner of the attic; he found nothing. The moans stopped and he went down. The moaning began again and went on for a couple of hours. Then it stopped, suddenly.

After two days he had a letter from his wife in the States which told him of the death of one of his little girls, aged eight years. [The letter said] that she'd asked for her father before dying.

This thing, it shows us that we can hear moans (or see drops of blood) to warn us before the death of another.

33   The Wizard's White Magic

There were some men who passed for wizards—Alexis Dulac and Grand Jacquot, of Saint-François (Beauce). They both feared each other. Each claimed to have more skill than the other in giving charms and making magic.

One day Alexis was threshing with the flail in his barn. When Grand Jacquot passed, he knew of this. He says to himself, "We must see today which of us two is the stronger." He goes into the barn and says: "Today we are going to see which of us two is the most powerful. Can you make the water of the Chaudière River come into your barn?" It was almost a hundred and fifty feet to the river from the barn.

Alexis replies, "I can't, nor can you either."

On this Grand Jacquot says, "You're going to see if I can't." Suddenly there is thunder, flashes of lightning, and the water of the Chaudière starts to get ruffled, to boil up, and flow toward the barn. It takes only an instant for the water to reach the barn door. The water comes into the barn.

When Alexis sees it in his threshing room, he climbs on the partition. Immediately the water reaches the partition. He climbs on the beam. When he was on the beam he looks outside the barn through the door; he sees that the water will soon be as high as the door. He says, "The cursed one is going to drown me in my barn." From the beam he takes a spring and dives into the threshing room. There isn't a drop of water. He just missed killing himself in the fall.

It was white magic. Dulac told this to his son; it's his son that I heard tell it, and also another son, Pierre Dulac.

34   Cadieux's Lament

I was speaking to you a moment ago about the wars with the Indians; now I'm going to tell you the story of a brave Canadian who played a great role in one of these wars.

Going up the great Ottawa River no one fails to stop at the Little Rock of the High Mountain in the middle of the Seven Falls portage, below Grand Calumet Island: there is the grave of Cadieux, of which everyone has heard.

Every time the company canoes pass the Little Rock an old voyageur tells the young men the story of Cadieux; the old voyageurs who have already heard it like to hear it again, when they don't retell it themselves. This time it was old Morache, an elderly guide, who unfolded to us the story of Cadieux's adventures.

Cadieux was a voyageur-interpreter married to an Algonquin woman; he usually spent the winter hunting and the summer dealing with the natives on behalf of the merchants. It was the time of the last Iroquois' expeditions: Cadieux had spent the hunting season at Seven Falls portage where he lived with some other families: it was then the month of May and Cadieux was waiting for the natives from the Island and the Courte-Oreille (Ottawas) who would be going down to Montreal with their furs at the same time as he.

The greatest peace reigned in the huts at Little Rock, when one fine day a young brave, who was roaming around the rapids and the lower portage, arrived all out of breath in the midst of the families scattered among the huts, and cried: "The Iroquois! The Iroquois!"

Apparently an Iroquois war party was at that moment only a league below the Seven Falls portage: they knew it was the time when the canoes went down the Grand River on their way from the hunting grounds, and they wished to attack.

There was only one way to escape: to try to run the rapids, a thing almost unheard of, for, as old Morache said, they are not thick and fast, the canoes that run the Seven Falls!

But that was not all, however: someone would have to stay to make a diversion, drawing the Iroquois into the woods, and stopping them from seeing what was happening once they began the portage. For those who know the Iroquois of that period will easily understand that, without such a stratagem, the sight of the fresh tracks left by the families would lead them immediately to split into two bands, one going up and the other down the river in pursuit of the fugitives.

Cadieux, as the most capable and expert of all, assumed the dangerous but unselfish mission, taking with him a young Algonquin in whose courage and loyalty he had perfect confidence. Their end achieved, Cadieux and his companion planned to take the surest road to rejoin their people, who would send to meet them if there was too much delay.

They left the cabins: once their preparations were made, Cadieux and his young companion, armed with their guns, axes, and knives, and furnished with some provisions, left to cut off the Iroquois. It was agreed that the canoes would leave the shelter of the river and shoot the rapids as soon as they heard the sound of rifle shots from the direction of the portage.

An hour had not passed before a rifle shot rang out, followed soon by another, then by several. During the struggle, in the noise of the shots, the canoes, caught up in the terrible currents, bounded through the bubbles and foam, plunged and rose on the crest of the waves that carried them into their course. The skilled oarsmen, men and women, at both ends of each canoe, guided their movements, avoiding the sharp points of the rocks, and held with their paddles those frail bark canoes in the most favourable stream of water shown by the state of the waves and the shape of the currents.

They had, on taking off, commended themselves to the good Sainte Anne, and they prayed most sincerely all the time.

"I saw nothing in the Seven Falls," later said Cadieux's wife, who was a pious woman, "I saw nothing but a noble Lady in white who hovered over the canoes and showed us the way!"

The canoes were saved and arrived in a few days beyond reach of their enemies at Two Mountains Lake. But what were Cadieux and his Indian doing during this time, and what became of them? This is what happened, as was learned much later from some Iroquois and the people sent to meet the brave interpreter.

Cadieux had first let the Iroquois enter the portage. After choosing the most favourable spot for keeping out of sight of the river, he lay in ambush a short distance from the path, well hidden in the thick bushes; he had at the same time hidden his companion on some higher ground to give the impression of several parties as the fighting went on.

Cadieux let pass the Iroquois scouts, who scanned the edge of the path, and the first warrior canoe-bearers. Then, the enemies having reached the spot where the young Algonquin was hidden, he heard the shot of the latter and the cry of a wounded enemy.

The Iroquois, thus suddenly attacked, jumped with surprise and stopped at once; but before the porters could even lay down their burdens, Cadieux fired a second shot into the midst of the train and struck down a second warrior.

Cadieux had probably arranged to meet his companion in a kind of small clearing, a little removed from the portage, for it is towards this spot that both headed after successfully firing from the shelter of the bushes.

The advantage with which the two brave men attacked their many enemies did not keep the young Algonquin from falling under their blows. He did not rejoin Cadieux at the rendezvous; but he sold his life dearly.

For three days the Iroquois beat the forest to find the tracks of the families, not even imagining that they had been able to go down the rapids; for three days also they tracked the brave voyageur in the woods. Three days and three nights that were without sleep or rest for the unfortunate Cadieux! At the end of that time the invaders, despairing of finding the families and of beating their elusive adversary, convinced that they had lost the advantage of their foray, turned their canoes to go back down the Grand River.

Several days had passed since the families had left Little Rock: they learned that the Iroquois had gone back, and Cadieux had not yet arrived. Three men set out then for the meeting place of the interpreter and his companion. The three voyageurs went back up the Ottawa right to the Portage of the Fort without finding any traces of what had happened; there they began to see signs of the Iroquois' passage, and above that signs that they recognized as showing that their friend had stayed in the vicinity.

When, arriving at the portage of the Seven Falls, they found a little shelter built of branches which seemed to have been abandoned, they resolved to push their search a little farther in case Cadieux and his companion had perhaps been obliged to go up the river to take refuge with the Island Indians.

Two days later, the thirteenth since Cadieux and the families separated, they retraced their steps after having consulted the Indians who met them, certain that their two friends were back at Two Mountains Lake or dead.

In passing again near the Little Rock, they saw, far away on the edge of the portage path, beside the little shelter that they had thought abandoned some days earlier, a wooden cross which they approached with respect mixed with a strange wonder.

The cross was planted at the head of a grave, scarcely hollowed out in the ground, and in this grave lay the still fresh corpse of Cadieux, half buried in green branches. The dead hands were crossed on his breast, on which lay a large sheet of birchbark covered with writing.

The voyageurs picked up this bark which could reveal to them the mystery of their friend's death and explain the extraordinary circumstances. One of them, who could read, read the words confided to this wooden paper, and re-read them several times, facing the scarcely cold body of the brave Cadieux.

From what they saw and what was written on the bark, the voyageurs concluded that poor Cadieux, his mind spent by fatigue, lack of sleep, anxiety, and privation, had ended, as is almost always the case in such circumstances by wandering blindly until he came back to the same place he had left. Once there, he had lain without plans, according to the phrase of old Morache, for several days, sustained by fruits and a little hunting, without making a fire in his little shelter for fear of the Iroquois, getting weaker from day to day. At the time they passed this spot two days earlier, he had recognized them after investigation, but the burst of joy gave him such a shock that he lay without word or movement. After they left, at last he lost hope. Feeling himself near to death and gathering a little strength in these solemn moments, he had, after writing his last farewell to the world of the living, prepared his sepulchre, set his cross on his tomb, placed himself in his grave, and heaped up over him as best he could the branches with which his body was covered, to wait thus, in prayer, the death that he knew could not be long in coming.

Cadieux was a voyageur, poet, and warrior; what he had written on the bark was his death chant. Before lying down in this cold tomb by the Seven Falls portage, the imagination of one who had so lived with nature was exalted, and, as he was accustomed to compose voyageur songs, he had written his last song on this wooden sheet.

He addressed himself first, in this death chant, to those who gathered round him, announcing his approaching end and his regrets in leaving life; then he speaks of his sufferings, of the anxiety he feels for the families that he had brought together in his care, whom he calls friends.

He speaks of his terrible fears at the sight of the smoke of a camp near his shelter, of his too great satisfaction in recognizing the French faces, of his powerlessness to call them and to dart forth toward them, of their departure without being aware of his presence, and of his desolation.

Cadieux sees a wolf and a crow coming to smell his sick body; by calling on the gaiety of the hunter and the pride of the forest warrior, he threatens one with his gun and tells the other to go feast on the corpses of the Iroquois he had killed.

He then charges the nightingale, companion of his sleepless nights, to carry his farewells to his wife and his children whom he loved so much; then, like the good Christian he is, he places himself in the hands of his Creator and commends himself to the protection of Mary.

Some voyageurs claimed that Cadieux did not know how to write and that the fact of this song written on the bark could be, consequently, only the result of a miracle, but Cadieux, without being educated, knew how to write like all the interpreters of that period. Always this thing has been seen as it is told.

Here is that lament of Cadieux which he wrote on bark at the Little Rock of the Seven Falls, after placing himself in the grave hollowed out by his own hands:

> Little rock on the high mountain,
> I come here to end this campaign.
> Ah, sweet echoes, hear my sighs!
> Languishing, I am soon going to die.

Little birds, your sweet harmonies
When you sing draw me again toward life.
Ah, if I had wings like you
I would be happy within two days!

Alone in these woods where I am worried,
Thinking always of my dearest friends,
I ask "Alas! are they drowned?
Have the Iroquois killed them?"

One of those days when I went away,
On returning I saw smoke;
I said to myself, "Ah, great God, what is that?
Have the Iroquois taken my home?"

I went a little to the side
To see if it was an ambush;
Then I saw three French faces
Which filled my heart with great joy!

My knees folded, my feeble voice stopped,
I fell down. Alas! they prepared to go away:
I remained alone . . . No one to console me
When death comes with such great desolation.

A howling wolf comes near my cabin
To see if my fire no longer crackles.
I tell him: "Go away from here
For by my faith I see your coat."

A black crow flying at random
Comes to perch beside my roof.
I tell him: "Eater of human flesh,
Go to look for other food than me.

"Go back there, in the woods and swamp
You will find several Iroquois bodies;
You will find some flesh, also some bone;
Go farther away, leave me in peace!"

Nightingale, go tell my wife,
Tell my children, that I take my leave of them,
That I have kept my love and my faith,
And henceforth they must give me up.

It is here then that the world abandons me,
But I have aid from you, Saviour of men!
Very Holy Virgin, ah, do not abandon me.
Allow me to die between your arms!

The three Canadians wept as they read the brave Cadieux's death chant on the bark. They strengthened the wooden cross, filled up the grave holding the remains of this great man, raised a mound over the solitary tomb, and prayed for the peace of their friend's soul.

The bark on which Cadieux's lament was written was taken to the Lake post; the voyageurs set an appropriate air to this song, so typical of the rude life of the hunter and forest warrior, so surprising in its thoughts and so worthy of note because of the circumstances of its composition.

They were in the habit of keeping a copy of the lament, as written on the bark, fastened to a tree near Cadieux's grave at the Seven Falls portage. This was still done in my time, and it is in the same spot that I learned Cadieux's story, of which the voyageurs are so proud.

35 The Chasse-Galerie

"Now I'm going to tell you an amazing story from beginning to end; but if there are among you some jolly fellows who've longed to run with the chasse-galerie or the loup-garou, I warn you that they'd do better to go outside to see if the witch cats hold their sabbath, for I'm going to begin my story by making the grand sign of the cross to chase the Devil and his imps. I've had enough of those cursed things in my youth."

* * *

Not a man looks like going out; on the contrary they all gather in the cookhouse where the cook finished his preamble and prepared to tell a story to fit the occasion. It was New Year's Eve, 1858, in the deep virgin forest in the shanties of Ross, up above the Gatineau. The season had been hard and the snow was already as high as the roof of the cabin.

The boss had, according to custom, ordered that a little barrel of rum be distributed among the shantyboys, and the cook had finished early preparing the stew for the next day's meal. The molasses boiled in the big kettle for the taffy pull which would wind up the party.

Everyone had filled his pipe with good Canadian tobacco and a thick cloud darkened the inside of the cabin where, at intervals, a crackling fire of resinous pine cast some rosy glimmers that flickered, lighting with some marvelous effects of half-light the male figures of the rustic woodsmen.

Joe the cook was a little rather ill-favoured man who was generally called "the hunchback" without him taking offence, and he had worked in the shanty for at least forty years. He'd played all sorts of tricks and had all kinds of experiences in his checkered career, and taking a little drink of rum was enough to loosen his tongue and cause him to tell about his adventures.

* * *

I'll tell you, then, he went on, that if I was a little rough in my youth I no longer listen to mockery of religious things. I go to confession regularly every year and what I'm going to tell you happened in the days of my youth when I feared neither God nor Devil. It was an evening like this, the last day of the year, when I was thirty-four or thirty-five. Gathered with my friends around the cookhouse, we took a little drink; but if little streams make great rivers, the little glasses ended by emptying great jugs, and in those days we were thirstier and drank more often than today, and it wasn't unusual to see the celebrations end with fist-fights and hair-pulling. The rum was good—not better than this evening—but it was good, I assure you.

I had indeed imbibed a dozen little glasses myself, and by eleven o'clock, I tell you frankly, my head was spinning and I fell on my sleigh-rug for a little sleep while waiting for the hour to dance around the boar's head from the old year into the new, as we are going to do tonight at midnight before going to sing in the New Year and offer best wishes to the men of the neighbouring shanty.

I was sleeping then for some time, when I felt myself rudely shaken by the boss of the lumberjacks who says to me, "Joe! Midnight has come and you're late for the square dance. The fellows are leaving for their trip, and me, I'm going to Lavaltrie to see my blonde. Do you want to come with me?"

"To Lavaltrie!" I replied. "Are you crazy? We're more than a hundred leagues from there, and besides, if you have two months to make the trip, there's no way to go in the snow. And there's work the day after New Year's."

"Dumbbell!" replied my friend. "Don't worry about that. We'll make the trip by rowing a bark canoe and tomorrow morning at six o'clock we'll be back in the shanty."

I understood. My friend suggested that I ride in the chasse-galerie and risk my eternal soul for the pleasure of going to kiss my sweetheart in the village. It was a bit steep. It was indeed true that I was a little drunk and dissolute and that religion didn't worry me at this time, but to risk selling my soul to the Devil, that was too much.

"Don't be chicken," continued Baptiste, "You know there's no danger. It's a question of going to Lavaltrie and returning in six hours. You know that with the chasse-galerie we travel at least fifty leagues in an hour when one can row like us. It's simply a question of not speaking the name of God during the journey and not getting caught on the crosses of steeples while travelling. That's easy to do and to avoid all danger you just have to think about what you say and watch where you're going, and not drink on the way. I've already made the trip five times and you see that I've never come to harm.

"Let's go, my old fellow! Take your courage in both hands and, if you're brave enough, in two hours we'll be in Lavaltrie. Think of little Liza Guimbette and of the pleasure of hugging her. We've already seven making the trip, but we have to have two, four, six, or eight, and you'll be the eighth."

"All that's very fine, but you have to make a promise to the Devil and he's a creature who doesn't put up with a change of heart when you pledge yourself to him."

"A simple formality, my Joe. It's simply a question of not getting drunk and paying attention to your speech and your rowing. A man isn't a child, what the devil! Come, come, our friends wait for us outside, and the big canoe for the drive is all ready for the trip."

I let myself be led out of the cabin where I saw six of our men waiting for us, a paddle in each hand. The big canoe was on the snow in a clearing and before I had time to reflect I was already seated in the front, the paddle hanging on the gunnel, waiting for the signal to leave. I confess that I was a little worried but Baptiste, who was known in the shanty for not going to confession for seven years, gave me no time to sort it out. He was standing in the stern and, in a ringing voice, he says to us: "Repeat with me," and we repeated:

"Satan! ruler of hell, we promise to give you our souls if from now until six o'clock we pronounce the name of your master and ours, the good God, and if we touch a cross during the trip. On these conditions, you will carry us through the air to the place where we wish to go and you will also bring us back to the shanty!

"*Acabris! Acabras! Acabram!*

Carry us over the mountains!"

Scarcely had we spoken the last words than we felt the canoe rise in the air to a height of five or six hundred feet. It seemed to me that I was light as a feather and under Baptiste's order we began to row like the madmen we were. At the first strokes of the paddles the canoe rose in the air like an arrow and, as the saying goes, the Devil carried us. It cut off our breath and our hair stood up in our fur caps. We flew faster than the wind.

For a quarter of an hour, nearly, we sailed above the forest without seeing anything but the clusters of the tall black pines.

It was a superb night and the full moon lighted the sky like a bright sun at midday. It was a stormy cold and our whiskers were covered with hoar frost, but we were all rowing. That's easy to understand, since it was the Devil who drove us, and I assure you that it wasn't on the path of the Virgin. We soon saw a clearing—it was the Gatineau River with the surface frozen and polished, sparkling below us like an enormous mirror.

Then, little by little, we saw some lights in the houses of the inhabitants; then the steeples of churches which shone like the bayonets of soldiers when they exercise on the field of Mars in Montreal. We passed these steeples as fast as one passes the telegraph poles when travelling by train. And we flew like all the devils, passing over villages, forests, rivers, and leaving them behind us like a trail of sparks. It's Baptiste the madman who steers us for he knows the way and we soon reach the Ottawa River which guides us to come down right at Two Mountains Lake.

"Wait a little!" cries Baptiste, "We're going to skirt Montreal and we're going to scare the gadabouts who are still outside their houses. You, Joe, there in front, clear your throat and let's sing a paddling song."

Indeed we saw already the thousand lights of the city and Baptiste, with a stroke of his oar, made us come down a little, even with the towers of Nôtre Dame. I took out my quid of tobacco, so I wouldn't swallow it, and I struck up loudly this special song which all the rowers repeated in chorus.

> My father had no child but me,
>   Bark canoe that's going to fly,
> One day he sent me off to sea,
>   Bark canoe that flies, that flies,
>   Bark canoe that's going to fly.
>
> One day he sent me off to sea,
>   Bark canoe that's going to fly,
> The man who took me off to sea—
>   Bark canoe that flies, that flies,
>   Bark canoe that's going to fly.

The man who took me off to sea—
   Bark canoe that's going to fly,
He said, "My dearest one, kiss me."
   Bark canoe that flies, that flies,
   Bark canoe that's going to fly.

He said, "My dearest one, kiss me."
Bark canoe that's going to fly,
"Oh no, sir, I don't dare kiss thee."
   Bark canoe that flies, that flies,
   Bark canoe that's going to fly.

"Oh no, sir, I don't dare kiss thee,
   Bark canoe that's going to fly,
"For if my father knew, ah me!
   Bark canoe that flies, that flies,
   Bark canoe that's going to fly.

"For if my father knew, ah me!
   Bark canoe that's going to fly,
A beaten daughter I'd soon be."
   Bark canoe that flies, that flies,
Bark canoe that's going to fly.

Although it was nearly two o'clock in the morning we saw some groups stop in the street to watch us pass, but we flew so fast that in the twinkling of an eye we'd by-passed Montreal and its suburbs. Then I began to count the steeples—Long Point, Pointe-aux-Trembles, Repentigny, St. Sulpice, and finally the two silver spires of Lavaltrie which dominated the green summit of the tall pines of the county.

"Watch! You others," cried Baptiste. "We're going to land at the edge of the wood in the field of my godfather, Jean-Jean Gabriel, and we'll return on foot to surprise our acquaintances at some drunken party or neighbourhood dance."

What was said was done, and five minutes later our canoe rested in a snowbank on the edge of Jean-Jean Gabriel's wood; and all eight of us went off in line to the village. It wasn't an easy task for there was no beaten track and we had snow right up to our asses. Baptiste, who was bolder than the others, went to knock on the door of his godfather's house where we saw some light. But he found only a hired girl who told him that the old people were at a snack at Father Robillard's but the boys and girls of the parish had nearly all gone to Batissette Augé's house in Petite Misère, below Contrecoeur, on the other side of the river, where they had a New Year's Party.

"Let's go to the party at Batissette's!" said Baptiste. "We're sure to find our girls."

"Let's go to Batissette's!"

And we went back to the canoe, warning ourselves against speaking certain words or taking a drop too much, for we had to retrace the route to the shanties and get there before six in the morning, otherwise we'd be roasted like sheep and the Devil would carry us to the deepest pit of hell.

"Acabris! Acabras! Acabram!
Carry us over the mountains!"

Baptiste cried again, and here we are on our way back to Petite-Misère, sailing through the air like the sinners we all were. In two strokes of the paddle we'd crossed the river and were carried to Batissette Augé's where the house was all lighted up. Faintly below we heard the sounds of a fiddle and the laughter of the dancers whose shadows we saw flitting about through the ice-coated window-panes. We hid our canoe behind the pile of frozen chunks that lined the bank, for the ice had piled up that year.

Now Baptiste repeated to us, "No mistakes, friends, and watch your words. Let's dance like lost souls, but not a single glass of beer or rum, you hear. And at the first sign, everyone follow me, for we must leave without attracting attention."

And we went to knock at the door.

Father Batissette came to open it himself and we were welcomed with open arms by the guests who knew most of us.

We were first greeted with questions: "Where did you come from?" "I thought you were in the shanties." "You come very late." "Come and take a drop."

It was Baptiste who got us out of trouble by starting to speak: "First let us take our hats off and then let us dance. We've come specially for that. Tomorrow morning I'll answer all your questions and tell you all you want to know."

As for me, I had already found Liza Guimbette who was going with little Boisjoli from Lanoraie. I went up to greet her and ask her for the next number which was a square dance. She accepted with a smile which made me forget that I'd risked my soul's salvation to have the pleasure of dancing about and living it up in her company.

For two hours one dance followed another and it isn't for me to boast if I tell you that at this time there wasn't my equal in ten towns around for the simple jig or the waltz. My friends, for their parts, amused themselves like good fellows and all I can tell you is that the farmer boys were tired of us when the clock struck four. I thought I saw Baptiste Durand going to the buffet where the men got their nips of white whiskey from time to time, but I was so busy with my partner that I didn't pay much attention.

But, now that the time to get into the canoe had come, I saw clearly that Baptiste had taken a drop too much and I had to take him by the arm to make him go out with me, signaling to the others to get ready to follow us without attracting the dancers' attention. We went out one after the other without drawing any notice, and five minutes later we had climbed into the canoe, having left the dance like Indians without saying goodbye to anyone; not even to Liza whom I'd asked to dance a special number. I've always thought that was why she decided to ditch me and marry little Boisjoli without even inviting me to the wedding, the little sneak.

But to return to our canoe, I tell you that we were awfully annoyed to see that Baptiste Durand had had a drink, for it was he who steered us and we had just enough time to get back to the shanty by six in the morning before the men who weren't working wakened on New Year's Day. The moon had disappeared and it was no longer as clear as before, and it wasn't without fear that I took my place at the front of the canoe, determined to keep an eye on the route we were going to follow. Before we rose into the air I turned and said to Baptiste, "Watch it! Look, old man! Head for the Montreal mountain as soon as you see it."

"I know my business," replied Baptiste, "and you mind yours."

And before I had time to reply . . .

"Acabris! Acabras! Acabram!
Carry us over the mountain!"

And there we were returning at full speed. But it soon became clear that our pilot no longer had as sure a hand, for the canoe described some uneasy zigzags. We passed not a hundred feet from the clock of Contrecoeur, and instead of guiding us to the west toward Montreal, Baptiste made us follow the roads toward the Richelieu River. Some instants later we passed over Beloeil Mountain and the front of the canoe was within ten feet of breaking on the great temperance cross that the Bishop of Quebec had set up there.

"To the right, Baptiste, to the right, my old one, for you're sending us to the devil if you don't steer better than that!"

And Baptiste instinctively turned the canoe to the right, setting the course on the Montreal mountain that we already saw in the distance. I confess that fear began to run through us, we'd be burnt like young pigs that are roasted after butchering. And I swear that the accident wasn't long in coming. For, at the moment we passed over Montreal, Baptiste made us sheer and, before we had time to prepare, the canoe landed in a snowbank in a clearing on the mountainside.

Happily it was in soft snow so nobody was hurt, and the canoe wasn't smashed. But scarcely were we out of the snow than Baptiste began to swear like one possessed and to declare that before starting back for the Gatineau he'd go down to the village and get a drink. I tried to reason with him, but how can you talk sense to a drunkard who wants to wet his whistle? Then, at the end of patience, and rather than surrender our souls to the Devil who was already licking his chops on seeing us in trouble, I said a word to my other companions, who were as scared as I. And we all turned on Baptiste, whom we threw down without hurting him, and we put him in the bottom of the canoe after tying him like a piece of sausage and gagging him to prevent him saying the dangerous words when we were in the air.

And, *"Acabris! Acabras! Acabram!"*

There we were starting off again at the speed of all the devils, for we had no more than an hour to get to the Gatineau shanty. It's I who steered this time and I assure you that I kept my eyes open and my arm steady. We crossed the Ottawa River like a fish, right to Gatineau Point, and from there we turned north toward the shanty.

We'd gone no more than a few leagues when that dumbbell Baptiste, who had freed himself from the rope we'd tied him with and pulled out his gag, stood up in the canoe, letting out an oath that made my hair stand on end. It was impossible to struggle with him in the canoe without running the risk of falling from a height of two or three hundred feet, and the fool shook like a lost soul, threatening us all with the oar that he'd seized and which he whirled around our heads, making it twirl like an Irishman with a shillelagh. The situation was terrible as you can well understand.

Happily we were arriving, but I was so excited that I made a false move to dodge Baptiste's oar: the canoe hit the top of a tall pine and threw us all down, tumbling from branch to branch like a partridge that one kills in the spruce trees. I don't know how long I took falling right to the bottom for I lost consciousness before landing, and my last memory was like that of a man who dreams of falling into a bottomless pit.

Toward eight o'clock in the morning I woke in my bed in the cabin, carried there by some lumberjacks who had found us unconscious, buried right to the neck in a nearby snowbank. Happily no one had broken his back, but I don't need to tell you that I was bruised all over like a man who slept on rocks for a week, without mentioning a black eye and two or three cuts on my hands and face.

In short, the main thing is that the Devil hadn't carried us off, and I don't need to tell you that I wasn't eager to contradict those who pretended they'd found me with Baptiste and the six others all drunk as thrushes and sleeping off our rum in a snowbank nearby. It wasn't right to risk selling one's soul to the Devil and boast of it among the fellows, and it's only many years later that I told the story as it happened.

All I can tell you, friends, is that it isn't as funny as one thinks to go to see your girl in a bark canoe in the depth of winter, riding in the chasse-galerie, especially if you have a wild drunkard who interferes with the steering. If you believe me, wait till next summer to kiss your sweethearts. Then you won't run the risk of travelling with the Devil as helmsman.

* * *

And Joe the cook stuck his wooden spoon into the molasses, boiled to a golden glow, and declared that the taffy was done to a turn and it was ready for us to pull it.

The Informants

The tales Adélard Lambert collected present the largest group from a single source so some information on the Lambert family may be of interest. The following notes are translated and condensed from Gustave Lanctôt's account in the *Journal of American Folklore* in 1923.

The father, Jean-Baptiste Lambert, was born in 1821 in Berthier-en-haut, in the county of Berthier, Quebec. The son of farmers and himself a farmer, he settled on the land in Saint-Cuthbert in the same county. In 1844 he married Leocadie Rinfret who was born in 1825 in Maskinonge county which borders on Berthier. They had numerous children, of whom those still alive in 1923 were, with their birthdates: Honoré (1848), Joseph (1855), Georgianna (1857), Hormisdas (1859), Malvina (1863), Olivine (1865), Adélard (1867), and Marie-Louise (1869).

In 1869 M. Lambert emigrated to the United States, settling first in Wonsocket, Rhode Island, and later in Fall River, Massachusetts. In these little towns, factories then being built brought in a cosmopolitan population. After the work day in the mills, some of these immigrants would gather in groups in the town and kick up a row, often bullying and fighting with peaceful citizens. Hence families did not want their children to go out in the streets after supper. During those long evenings around the lamp, once the schoolwork was done, Madame Lambert would occupy and distract her many small children by telling them stories, posing riddles, singing songs, or teaching them rounds. It was thus that Adélard learned most of the stories in his collection. Madame Lambert had a pretty voice and a remarkable memory. In her youth during many pleasant gatherings in the country during the long Canadian winters she had heard a great many stories and songs, and she told them all to her children while they were growing up.

Adélard Lambert's collection included not only stories from his mother but from other members of his family, including his brother-in-law, Alexandre Poudrier, who grew up in the county of Saint-Maurice next to Maskinonge and enjoyed a reputation as a good storyteller. When he married M. Lambert's oldest daughter, he followed the Lamberts to the United States where young Adélard heard his stories. Another source was an elderly man known as "Father Bernier" who lived near the Lamberts in Rhode Island and told stories to Adélard when he was a boy of twelve.

Of the tales included in this book, Adélard attributed "The Bee and the Toad," "The Split Tuque," and "Three Annoying Tales" to his mother. "Give Me Back My Purse" and "The Calf with the Golden Horns" he attributed to his two youngest sisters, Marie-Louise and Olivine, who remembered them from their mother. "The Calf Sold Three Times" and "Two Neighbours" came from Alexandre Poudrier, and "The Carefree Miller" and "The Winter of the Crows" from old family friends.

Less information is available about the other storytellers, but Dr. Barbeau gave brief notes on the informants from whom he collected the tales he presented in the *Journal of American Folklore* in 1920.

François Saint-Laurent, who told of "The Loup-Garou of the Cemetery" and "The Three Drops of Blood," was a fisherman aged forty-nine in 1917. He lived in La Tourelle, Gaspé, and his language was characterized by the dialect peculiar to the northwest Gaspé. His paternal grandfather came from Rimouski; his grandfather and father were farmers and fishermen. His mother was a native of Sainte-Marie, Beauce. He told Dr. Barbeau that the tale of "The Loup-Garou of the Cemetery" came indirectly from Alexis Vallée, who told it to Saint-Laurent's father. In addition to the two stories named, he told three other loup-garou stories he heard from his grandparents, as well as two stories of the chasse-galerie.

Charles Barbeau, aged seventy-five in 1919, told the stories about "The Feu-Follet and the Knife" and "The Wizard's White Magic." A farmer and shopkeeper originally from Saint-François in Beauce county, Barbeau later settled in Sainte-Marie, Beauce. His father had lived for many years in Saint-Joseph; his mother, Catherine O'Brien, was Irish by birth and had emigrated to Canada with her parents while very young.

Alcide Léveillé, who told of "The Black Dog at Le Rocher-Malin," was an old farmer aged seventy-three in 1917, living at Notre-Dame-du-Portage, Témiscouata. His father was a native of Ecureuils, Portneuf, and his mother of Rivière-du-Loup, Témiscouata.

Whatever is known of the other storytellers is incorporated in the notes on their stories.

The following list gives the names of the informants, followed by the numbers of their tales.

Barbeau, Charles, 30, 33
Boulet, Angèle, 25
Caron, Widow, 24
Dupuis, Hermias, 31
Fournier, Achille, 1, 7
Lambert, Mme J.-B., 9, 21, 22, 23, 27
Lambert, Marie-Louise, 2
Lambert, Olivine, 3
Landry, Hélène, 19
Léveillé, Alcide, 26
Mantha, Felix, 6, 12
Morache, 34
Nazaire, 11
Patry, Paul, 4
Picard, George, 8
Poudrier, Alexandre, 15, 16
Rousselle, Joseph, 5
Saint-Laurent, François, 29, 32
Sanschagrin, Mme Édouard, 13, 14
Sioui, Mme Prudent, 10, 18
Sioui, Prudent, 17

Sources and References

Preface

The statement by Luc Lacourcière is from the *Journal of American Folklore*, 74(1961), 274. (The *Journal* is henceforth abbreviated to *JAF*.) Gustave Lanctôt's comment on Adélard Lambert's tales: *JAF*, 36(1923), 209.

Dr. Cloutier's statement: *JAF*, 33(1920), 278-79; Dr. Barbeau's comment: *JAF*, 33(1920), 273.

The Informants

Gustave Lanctôt's notes on the Lambert family: *JAF*, 36(1923), 205-9.

Barbeau's notes on Saint-Laurent, Charles Barbeau, and Alcide Léveillé: *JAF*, 33(1920), 174-75.

The Tales

The Stith Thompson quotations in the introductions to various sections are from *The Folktale* (New York: Holt, Rinehart & Winston, 1946): "Animal Tales," pp. 221 and 223; "Ordinary Folktales," p. 444; "Jokes and Anecdotes," p. 190; and "Formula Tales," p. 229.

The following notes on the individual tales give the source of each tale translated, list the relevant tale types and motifs, and cite some comparative references. Where references are abbreviated, the full listing can be found in the bibliography.

1   The Fable of the Bear and the Fox

Translated from "La Fable de l'ours et du renard," collected by Marius Barbeau from Achille Fournier, August, 1915, in Saint-Anne, Kamouraska. He learned it a long time earlier from Édouard Lizotte, also of Sainte-Anne. *JAF*, 30(1917), 113-14.

Margaret Low translated another French-Canadian version, "The Tub of Butter," which appears in Richard M. Dorson's *Folktales Told around the World*, pp. 445-48. She notes that "Type 15 is one of the best known animal tales in the French folklore of North America. Thirty-six versions of this theme have been collected to date: twenty from French Canada (Acadia 11, Quebec 9) where the protagonists are the fox and the wolf; and sixteen versions from Franco-America (Louisiana 13, Missouri 13) which are based on the rivalry between Lapin and Bouki."

Type AT 15, *The Theft of Butter (Honey) by Playing Godfather*. Motifs: K372, Playing godfather; K401.1, Dupe's food eaten and then blame fastened on him.

2   Give Me Back My Purse

Translated from "Rendez-moi ma bourse," collected by Adélard Lambert from Marie-Louise Lambert, communicated to Marius Barbeau, and prepared for publication by Gustave Lanctôt. *JAF*, 36(1923), 239-41.

No tale type is very close, but it resembles AT 210, *Hen, Duck, Pin, and Needle on a Journey*. Somewhat similar motifs include B296, Animals go a-journeying; K1161, Animals hidden in various parts of a house attack owner with their characteristic powers and kill him when he enters.

3 The Calf with the Golden Horns

Translated from "Les Cornes d'or," collected by Adélard Lambert from Olivine Lambert, communicated to Marius Barbeau, and prepared for publication by Gustave Lanctôt. *JAF*, 36(1923), 243-51.

This is a form of AT 314, *The Youth Transformed to a Horse*, and includes motifs G205, Witch stepmother; D133.4, Transformation: man to calf; B313, Helpful animal an enchanted person; S31, Cruel stepmother; D672, Obstacle flight; D700, Person disenchanted; D719, Disenchantment by rough treatment; L161, Lowly hero marries princess.

4 Ti-Jean and the Big White Cat

Translated from "Ti-Jean et la chatte blanche," collected by Marius Barbeau from Paul Patry, August 1914, at Saint-Victor, Beauce. M. Patry had learned it from his mother. *JAF*, 29(1916), 45-49.

This is a form of AT 402, *The Mouse (Cat, Frog, etc.) as Bride*, and includes motifs H1210.1, Quest assigned by father; H1308, Quest for finest of horses; B422, Helpful cat; H1306, Quest for the finest of linen; H1301, Quest for the most beautiful of women; D700, Person disenchanted; B313, Helpful animal an enchanted person; H1242, Youngest brother alone succeeds in quest; L10, Victorious youngest son.

5 Fearless Pierre

Translated from "Pierre sans peur," collected by Gustave Lanctôt from Joseph Rousselle who had learned it in his youth from his father in St. Denis, Kamouraska. *JAF*, 39(1926) 383-87.

It has some elements in common with AT 326, *The Youth Who Wanted to Learn What Fear Is*, and includes AT 326A, *Soul Released from Torment*. Motifs include L111.3, Widow's son as hero; Q82, Reward for fearlessness; H1411, Fear test: staying in a haunted house; E373.1, Money received from ghosts as reward for bravery; E334.2.1, Ghost of murdered person haunts burial spot; E338, Non-malevolent ghost haunts house or castle; E412.3, Dead without proper funeral rites cannot rest; E413, Murdered person cannot rest in grave; E415.1.2, Return from dead to uncover secretly buried treasure; L161, Lowly hero marries princess.

6 Poucet and Marie

Translated from "Poucet et Marie," collected by Mlle Bertha Mantha in October 1930 from her father Felix Mantha of Saint-Joseph d'Orleans who had heard it in his youth; published by Gustave Lanctôt. *JAF*, 44(1931), 234.

"The Twa Sisters" is Child 10; "Le Petit Doight enchanté," *JAF*, 44(1931), 252-55. Cf. Briggs B2, pp. 448-51.

AT 780: *The Singing Bone*. Motifs: E632.1: Speaking bones of murdered person reveal murder; H57.2.1, Severed finger as sign of crime; N270, Crime inevitably comes to light; Q210, Crimes punished.

7 The Three Golden Hairs

Translated from "Les Trois Poils d'or," collected by Marius Barbeau from Achille Fournier at Sainte-Anne, Kamouraska in July 1915. M. Fournier remembered this story from having heard it only once nearly forty years earlier from a French Canadian in Massachusetts. *JAF*, 30(1917), 123-25.

AT 882, *The Wager on the Wife's Chastity.* Motifs: N15, Chastity wager; T210, Faithful wife; K210.1, Calumniated wife; K2112.1, False tokens of woman's unfaithfulness; S432, Cast-off wife thrown in water; K1837, Disguise of woman in man's clothes; K1825, Disguise as professional man; S451, Outcast wife at last united with husband; Q210, Crimes punished.

Other French-Canadian versions include "Jean Cuit," *JAF*, 30(1917), 114-23; "La Femme en derive," *JAF*, 39(1926), 403-7; Soeur Marie-Ursule, "L'Etoile d'or," pp. 242-45; Carmen Roy, *Littérature orale en Gaspésie*, p. 228.

8 The Carefree Miller
Translated from "Le Meunier sans-souci," collected by Adélard Lambert from Georges Picard of Drummondville, communicated to Marius Barbeau and prepared by Pierre Daviault. *JAF*, 53(1940), 105-7. (See also Barbeau: *Les Contes du Grand-Père Sept-Heures*, 7, pp. 3-10)

It includes both AT 1004, *Hogs in the Mud; Sheep in the Air*, and AT 922, *The Shepherd Substituting for the Priest Answers the King's Questions*. Motifs: K404.1, Tails in ground; H541.1, Riddle propounded on pain of death; H681.3, Riddle: what is the center of the earth? H711.1, Riddle: what am I (the king) worth?, H524.1, Test: guessing person's thoughts; H561.4, King and clever youth; L161, Lowly hero marries princess. Cf. Briggs, A2, pp. 119-20; Marie-Ursule, pp. 254-55.

9 The Split Tuque
Translated from "La Tuque percée," collected by Adélard Lambert from his mother, Mme. J.-B. Lambert, communicated to Marius Barbeau, and prepared for publication by Gustave Lanctôt. *JAF*, 36(1923), 214-16.

This is a version of AT 1187, *Unfinished Work: Man to belong to the devil when work is finished.* Motifs: N251, Person pursued by misfortune; M210, Bargain with devil; G303.16.19.3, One is freed if he can set a task the devil cannot perform; H1020, Impossible tasks; K210, Devil cheated of his promised soul.

10 The Devil and the Candle
Translated from "Le Diable et la bougie," collected by Marius Barbeau at Lorette August 1914 from Mme Prudent Sioui who had learned it from her stepfather Clement Sioui. *JAF*, 29(1916), 110-11.

This resembles AT 1187*, *Meleager: Permission to live as long as candle lasts.* Motifs: M210, Bargain with devil; S241, Child unwittingly promised: "First thing you meet"; D1381.11, Magic circle protects from devil; K551.9, "Let me live as long as this candle lasts"; S250, Saving the promised child; K210, Devil cheated of his promised soul.

Cf. Briggs, Bl, pp.45, 53, 68-70, 76.

11 Dalbec Flies through the Air
Told by Nazaire, printed by William Parker Greenough in Chapter 4, pp. 249-50 of *Canadian Folk-Life and Folk-Lore* (New York: George H. Richmond, 1897).

AT 1881, *The Man Carried through the Air by Geese* (X1258.1)

12 The Pumpkin Seller
Translated from "Le Vendeur de citrouilles," collected by Mlle Berthe

Mantha in October 1930 from her father, Felix Mantha, in Saint Joseph d'Orleans, Ontario, where he had heard it in his youth. *JAF*, 44(1931), 232.

AT 1319, *Pumpkin Sold as an Ass's Egg*. Motifs: J1772.2.1, Pumpkin thought to be an ass's egg; J1902, Absurd ignorance concerning hatching of eggs.

Cf. Briggs, A2, pp. 120, 175; Barbeau, *JAF*, 28(1915), 95; Waugh, *JAF*, 31(1917), 78.

13 The Cobbler
Translated from "Le Cordonnier," collected by Soeur Marie-Ursule from Mme Édouard Sanschagrin and published in *Civilization traditionnelle des Lavalois*, pp. 267-68.

AT 1351, *The Silence Wager* (J2511). "Get Up and Bar the Door" is Child 275.

14 The Lousy-Head
Translated from "Le Pouilleux," collected by Soeur Marie-Ursule from Mme Édouard Sanschagrin and published in *Civilization traditionnelle des Lavalois*, pp. 266-67.

AT1365C, *The Wife Insults the Husband as Lousy-head*; Motif T255.3, The obstinate wife: Sign of the louse.

Cf. Halpert, p. 48.

15 Two Neighbours
Translated from "Les Deux Voisins," collected by Adélard Lambert from Alexandre Poudrier, communicated to Marius Barbeau, and prepared for publication by Gustave Lanctôt. *JAF* 36(1923), 252-53.

This incorporates elements of AT 1525, *The Master Thief*, and AT 1525H, *Thieves Steal from Each Other*. Motifs: K301, Master thief; K341.6, Shoes dropped to distract owner's attention; K341.7, Animal's cry imitated to distract owner's attention from his goods; J1510, The cheater cheated; Q552.18, Punishment: disappearance of ill-gotten gains.

Cf. Briggs, A2, pp. 413-18.

16 The Calf Sold Three Times
Translated from "Le Veau vendu trois fois," collected by Adélard Lambert from Alexandre Poudrier, communicated to Marius Barbeau, and prepared for publication by Gustave Lanctôt. *JAF*, 36(1923), 253-55.

AT 1585, *The Lawyer's Mad Client* (K1655).

Thomas Edward Oliver discusses "Some Analogues of Maestro Pierre Pathelin" in *JAF*, 22(1909), 395-430. W. J. Wintemberg gives a version told by his father in *Folklore of Waterloo County, Ontario*, p. 61. For an English version see Briggs A2, p. 235. Dr. Briggs notes that there are 59 Irish versions.

17 Richard's Cards
Translated from "Les Cartes du nommé Richard," collected by Marius Barbeau from Prudent Sioui of Lorette August 1914, as learned from his father. *JAF*, 29(1916), 134.

(M. Sioui did not remember what the "nine" stood for; other versions give it as "the nine ungrateful lepers.")

AT 1613, "*Playing Cards Are My Calendar and Prayerbook.*" Motif H603, Symbolic interpretation of playing cards.

"La Chanson des cartes," Frère Anselme et Père Daniel, *Chansons d'Acadie*, II, pp. 1-2.

18. The Dreams of the Hunters

Translated from "Le Rêve des chausseurs," collected by Marius Barbeau from Mme Prudent Sioui, Lorette, in August 1914. She had heard an old woman, Marie Bastien of Lorette, tell it a long time ago. *JAF*, 29(1916), 134-35.

AT 1626, *Dream Bread* (K444). Paul Franklin Baum discusses the history of this tale from 1106 on, and its distribution throughout Europe and Asia in *JAF*, 30(1917), 378-410. In *JAF*, 32(1919), 178-80, Dr. Barbeau questions Mr. Baum's theories about the origin of the Canadian versions and cites four more Canadian texts: two French-Canadian and two English-Canadian. Fauset gives still another Canadian version in *Folklore of Nova Scotia*, p. 54. Briggs gives two English versions, A2, pp. 264 and 297, and notes that there are 42 Irish versions.

19 The Little Mouse and the Little Fire-Coal

Translated from "La Petite Souris et le petit charbon de feu," collected by Malvina Tremblay from Hélène Landry, Ottawa, aged twelve, who learned it four years earlier from her grandmother, the widow L.-H. Tremblay, who was born in La Malbaie, Charlevoix, about 1831, and later lived in Chicoutimi. *JAF*, 32(1919), 110-12.

This is mainly Type AT 2034A, *Mouse Bursts Open when Crossing a Stream* (Z41.4.1), but it also includes elements of AT 135, *Mouse Makes a Boat of a Bread Crust* (B295.1), and AT 295, *The Bean, the Straw, and the Coal*, with motifs F1025.1, Bean, straw and coal go journeying, and A2741.1, Bean laughs till it splits.

20. Jean Barbeau

Translated from "Jean Baribeau" in "Facéties et contes canadiens," collected by Victor Morin. *JAF*, 30(1917), 146.

This comes under AT 2320, *Rounds: Stories which begin over and over again and repeat* (Z17).

21-23 A Catch Tale, an Unfinished Tale, and an Endless Tale

Translated from "Contes énnuyants," collected by Adélard Lambert from his mother, Mme Jean-Baptiste Lambert, around 1880 and communicated to Marius Barbeau. *JAF*, 44(1931), 261-62. The same tales are repeated in *JAF*, 53(1940), 156-57.

The first comes under AT 2200, *Catch Tales*, and somewhat resembles Z13.1, Catch tale: tale teller frightens listener: yells boo at exciting point.

The second comes under AT 2250, *Unfinished Tales* (Z12).

The third is AT 2301, *Corn Carried away Grain at a time* (Z11.1).

24 The Devil at the Dance

Translated from "Le Diable à la dance," communicated to Marius Barbeau by Dr. J.-E.-A. Cloutier in 1919, from people in l'Islet, especially the octogenarian widow of Joseph Caron; prepared for publication by A. Godbout and Jules Tremblay. *JAF*, 33(1920), 274-78.

Motifs: G303.1.2, The devil as a well-dressed gentleman; G303.5,

How the devil is dressed; G303.6.2.1, Devil appears at dance; G303.7.1.1, Devil rides a black horse; G303.16.3.1, Devils driven away by cross; G303.16.7, Devil is chased by holy water; and G303.17.2.7, Devil disappears amid terrible rattle.

A. Godbout notes variants locating the story in Petite-rivière-Saint-François, Saint-Pierre, and Saint-Isadore, Dorchester, *JAF*, 33(1920), 273-74, and Soeur Marie-Ursule gives three short versions that she collected in Sainte-Brigette de Laval, pp. 187-88. In an article in *Le Bulletin des Recherches historiques*, 5(1899), 100-4, Hubert LaRue summarized the popular beliefs on the subject.

25 The Devil as a Builder of Churches
Translated from "Le Cheval diabolique et la caverne du monument," communicated to Marius Barbeau by Dr. J.-E.-A. Cloutier March 1919, who had heard it from Angèle Boulet at L'Islet some thirty years earlier. *JAF*, 33(1920), 278-85.

Dr. Barbeau noted that the story of Satan as a builder of a church was also localized in Trois-Pistoles, Témiscouata, Saint-Augustin, Portneuf, and Saint-Michel, Bellechasse. Soeur Marie-Ursule adds references for Saint-Laurent, Saint-Augustin, and Sault-au-Recollet, and gives a short tale from Sainte-Claire, Dorchester, p. 186.

Motifs: V250 Virgin Mary; V510, Religious visions; G303.3.3.1.3, Devil as horse; D1209.1, Magic bridle; G303.9.1.6, Devil as builder of churches; D722, Disenchantment by taking off bridle; G303.9.9, Pranks played by the devil; G303.16.14, The devil exorcised; D1031.1.1, Consecrated bread as magic object.

26 The Black Dog at Le Rocher-Malin
Translated from "Le Chien noir, au Rocher-malin," collected by Marius Barbeau July 1918 at Notre-Dame-du-Portage from Alcide Leveillé, who had heard it sixty years earlier. *JAF*, 33(1920), 193-94.

Motifs: G303.3.9, Pranks played by the devil; G303.3.3.1.1, Devil in form of a dog.

27 The Bee and the Toad
Translated from "L'Abeille et le crapaud," collected by Adélard Lambert from Mme J.-B. Lambert, and prepared for publication by Gustave Lanctôt. *JAF*, 36(1923), 221-22.

Motif A2286.2, Animal characteristics result of contest between God and the devil.

28. The Winter of the Crows
Translated from "L'Hiver des corneilles," collected by Adélard Lambert, communicated to Marius Barbeau, and prepared by Pierre Daviault. *JAF*, 53(1940), 160-61.

Motif: A2234.1.1, Raven does not return to ark in obedience to Noah; black color is resulting punishment.

29 The Loup-Garou of the Cemetery
Translated from "Le Loup-garou de cimetière," collected by Marius Barbeau from François Saint-Laurent of La Tourelle, Gaspé, August 1918. *JAF*, 33(1920), 211-12.

Motifs: D1113.1.1, Transformation: man to werewolf; H64.1, Recognition of disenchanted person by thread in his teeth; G303.3.3.1.1,

Devil in form of dog.

Cf. "The Big Dog," Dorson, *Tales Told around the World*, pp. 463-64; Dorson, *Bloodstoppers*, pp. 71-78; *JAF*, 53(1940), 159;

Marie-Ursule, six versions, pp. 195-98; Harold W. Thompson, pp. 116-17.

30 The Feu-Follet and the Knife

Translated from "Le Feu-follet et le couteau," collected by Marius Barbeau March 1918 from Charles Barbeau who told him that "This little episode happened in Saint-Francois, Beauce, more than sixty years ago." *JAF*, 33(1920), 201.

Motifs: F401.2, Luminous spirits; F481.1, Will-o'-the-wisp leads people astray; F491.3.2, Power of will-o'-the-wisp neutralized if person sticks his knife in the ground; E742.1, Soul as will-o'-the-wisp.

Another story appears in *JAF*, 53(1940), 159, and Soeur Marie-Ursule quotes four short reports, pp. 190-91.

31 The Lutin and the Quail

Translated from "Le Lutin et la poule caille," collected by Marius Barbeau from Hermias Dupuis in Sainte-Marie, Beauce, June 1919. *JAF*, 33(1920), 184-85.

Motifs: F366.2.1, Fairies plait manes and tails of horses; F381, Getting rid of fairies. Cf. F405.6, Grain scattered as means of dispersing spirits.

Other accounts: Marie-Ursule, p. 199; Fraser, pp. 70-71; Dorson, *Bloodstoppers*, pp. 78-79; Beaugrand, *New Studies*, pp. 9-22.

32 The Three Drops of Blood

Translated from "Les Trois Gouttes de sang," collected by Marius Barbeau from François Saint-Laurent in La Tourelle, Gaspé, August 1918. *JAF*, 33(1920), 239-40.

Motifs: D1812.5.1.1.1, Tears of blood as evil omen; D1812.5, Future learned through omens; E281.3, Ghost haunts particular room in house; E402.1.1.2, Ghost moans.

33 The Wizard's White Magic

Translated from "La Magic blanche du sorcier,," collected by Marius Barbeau from Charles Barbeau, Sainte-Marie, Beauce, March 1915. *JAF*, 33(1920), 221.

Motifs: D1719.1, Contest in magic; D2031, Magic illusion.

34 Cadieux's Lament

Translated from Joseph-Charles Taché, *Forestiers et voyageurs* (Quebec, 1863; rpt. Montréal: Fides, 1946), chapter XV, pp. 134-42.

J.-C. Taché (1820-1894) was a doctor who became professor of physiology at Laval University, member of the Lower Canada House of Assembly, and founder of *Les soirées canadiennes*, a literary magazine in which the sketches and tales that make up *Forestiers et voyageurs* first appeared in 1863. Ernest Gagnon quoted Taché's story in *Chansons populaires du Canada* (1865), pp. 200-5, and Marius Barbeau repeated it in "La Complainte de Cadieux, coureur de bois (ca. 1709)," *JAF*, 67(1954), 168-83, where he lists thirteen different versions of the song and cites a study by Louvigny de Montigny who concluded that the hero of the legend was Jean Cadieu, who was born in Montreal or Boucherville March 12, 1671, and died in May 1709 at the age of thirty-eight.

35 The Chasse-Galerie

Translated from *La Chasse-Galerie: Légendes canadiennes* by Honoré Beaugrand (1900; rpt. Montréal: Fides, 1973), pp. 19-32.

Motifs: M210, Bargain with devil; D2122, Journey with magic speed; D2135, Magic air journey; F1021, Extraordinary flights through air.

Short accounts of the Chasse-galerie: *JAF*, 33(1920), 198-200; Harold W. Thompson, pp. 117-18; Dorson, *Bloodstoppers*, pp. 80-81; Marie-Ursule, pp. 185-86.

Index of Tale Types

The type numbers are from *The Types of the Folktale* by Antti Aarne and Stith Thompson (Folklore Fellows Communications 184, Helsinki, 1961).

Index of Motifs

Motif numbers are from Stith Thompson: *Motif-Index of Folk Literature*, 6 vols. (Bloomington: University of Indiana Press, 1955-1958).

Bibliography: French-Canadian Folktales

(Asterisks indicate the sources of tales in this collection.)

Arsenault, Georges. "La Marleche (conte-type 56B)." *Culture & Tradition,* 1(1976), 19-32.

Aubry, Claude. *The Magic Fiddler and Other Legends of French Canada.* Translated by Alice Kane. Toronto: Peter Martin, 1968.

——. *Le Violon magique et autres légendes du Canada français.* Ottawa: Deux rives, 1968.

*Barbeau, C. Marius. "Anecdotes de Gaspé, de la Beauce et de Témiscouata." *JAF,* 33(1920), 173-258.

——. *L'Arbre des rêves.* Montréal: Lumen, 1948.

——. "La Belle-Jarretière-verte, conte populaire." *Bulletin du Parler français* (Québec), 15(1916), 8-19.

——. "La Complainte de Cadieux, coureur de bois (ca. 1709)." *JAF,* 67(1954), 163-83.

——. "Contes de Charlevoix et de Chicoutimi." *JAF,* 32(1919), 112-67.

——. *Les Contes du Grand-Père Sept-Heures.* 12t. Montréal: Chantecler, 1950-1953.

——. "Contes populaires canadiens." *JAF,* 29(1916), 1-136; 30(1917), 1-140.

——. *Grand'mère raconte . . .* Montréal: Beauchemin, 1935.

——. *Il était une fois . . .* Montréal: Beauchemin, 1935.

——. "Les Métamorphoses dans les contes populaires canadiens." *Transactions of the Royal Society of Canada,* 10(1916), sec. 1, pp. 143-60.

——. "Notes sur la facétie des trois rêves." *JAF,* 32(1919), 178-80.

——. *Les Rêves des chasseurs.* Montréal: Beauchemin, 1942.

——. "La Tête, conte populaire." *Bulletin du Parler français,* 15(1917), 250-61.

——. *The Tree of Dreams.* Toronto: Oxford, 1955.

Barbeau, C. Marius, and Michael Hornyansky. *The Golden Phoenix and Other French-Canadian Fairy Tales.* Toronto: Oxford, 1958.

Barter, Geraldine. " 'Sabot-Bottes et P'tite Galoche': A Franco-Newfoundland Version of AT 505, The Cat as Helper." *Culture & Tradition,* 1(1976), 5-17.

Beaugrand, Honoré. *La Chasse-Galerie and Other Canadian Stories.* Montréal: Pelletier, 1900.

*——. *La Chasse-Galerie: Légendes canadiennes.* 1898; rpt. Montréal: Fides, 1973.

——. "Lutins in the Province of Quebec." *JAF,* 5(1892), 327-28.

——. *New Studies in Canadian Folklore.* Montréal: Renouf, 1904.

Bernier, Hélène. *La Fille aux mains coupées* (conte-type 706). Québec: Presses de l'université Laval, Archives de Folklore 12, 1971.

Beaubin, Charles-P. "Satan, constructeur des églises." *Bulletin des Recherches historiques,* 5(1899), 245-47.

Bolduc, Evelyn. "Un conte de la Beauce." *JAF,* 29(1916), 37-40.

——. "Contes de la Beauce." *JAF,* 32(1919), 90-101.

Boswell, Hazel. *Legends of Quebec*. Toronto: McClelland & Stewart, 1966.

Carlson, Natalie Savage. *The Talking Cat and Other Stories of French Canada*. New York: Harper, 1952.

Casgrain, Henri-Raymond. *La Jongleuse: Légende canadienne*. Montréal: Beauchemin, 1922.

_____. *Les Pionniers canadiens et le tableau de la Rivière Quelle: légendes*. Montréal: Beauchemin, 1861.

Chiasson, Anselme. *Les Légendes des Iles-de-la-Madeleine*. Moncton: Aboiteux, 1969.

*Cloutier, J.-E.-A. "Anecdotes de l'Islet." *JAF*, 33(1920), 273-94.

*Daviault, Pierre. "Contes populaires canadiens." *JAF*, 53(1940), 91-162.

De Gaspé, Philippe-Aubert, fils. *L'Influence d'un livre*. Québec: William Cowan, 1837; rpt., *Le Chercheur de trésor ou l'influence d'un livre*. Québec: Desbarats, 1864.

De Gaspé. Philippe-Aubert, père. *Les Anciens Canadiens*. Québec: Desbarats & Derbishire, 1863.

_____. *Canadians of Old*. Translated by C. G. D. Roberts. 1890; rpt. Toronto: McClelland & Stewart, 1974.

Doering, J. Frederick. "Legends from Canada, Indiana, and Florida." *Southern Folklore Quarterly*, 2(1938), 215-20.

Dorson, Richard M. "Canadiens." *Bloodstoppers and Bearwalkers*. Cambridge: Harvard University Press, 1959, 69-102.

_____. "Canadiens in the Upper Peninsula of Michigan." *Archives de Folklore*, 4(1950), 17-27.

Doucet, Alain. *La Littérature orale de la Baie Sainte-Marie*. Québec: Ferland, 1965.

Dupont, Jean-Claude. *Contes de bûcherons*. Montréal: Quinze, 1976.

_____. *Le Légendaire de la Beauce*. Québec: Garneau, 1974.

Gagnon, Alphonse. "La Facétie des 'Trois rêves": une autre version canadienne." *JAF*, 33(1920), 373.

Gallant, Melvin. *Ti-Jean, contes acadiens*. Moncton: Éditions d'Acadie, 1973.

Greenough, William Parker. "Amusements—Contes and Raconteurs." *Canadian Folk-Life and Folk-Lore*. New York: George H. Richmond, 1897, 45-66.

Haden, Ernest F. " 'La petite Cendrillouse.' Version acadienne de 'Cendrillon.' Étude linguistique." *Archives de Folklore*, 3(1948), 21-34.

Huston, James P. *Légendes canadiennes*. Paris, 1853.

Jolicoeur, Catherine. *Le Vaisseau fantôme: Légende étiologique*. Québec: Presses de l'université Laval, Archives de Folklore 11, 1970.

Lacourcière, Luc. *Le Catalogue raisonné du conte populaire français en Amerique du Nord*. 6 tomes en chantier.

_____. "Les échanges avantageux (conte-type 1655)." *Cahiers des Dix*, 35(1970), 227-50.

_____. "L'Horoscope, conte acadien." *Culture vivante* (Québec), 9(1968), 48-43.

_____. *Oral Tradition: New England and French Canada*. Québec: Archives de Folklore, Université Laval, 1972.

——. "Une pacte avec le diable (conte-type 361)." *Cahiers des Dix*, 37(1972)

——. "The Present State of French-Canadian Folklore Studies." *JAF*, 74(1961), 373-82.

——. "Le ruban qui rend fort (conte-type 590)." *Cahiers des Dix*, 36(1971), 235-97.

——. "Le triple destin de Marie-Josephte Corriveau (1733-1763)." *Cahiers des Dix*, 33(1968), 213-42; "Le destin posthume de la Corriveau." *ibid.*, 34(1969), 239-71; "Presence de la Corriveau." *ibid*, 38(1973), 228-64.

Lacourcière, Luc, and Margaret Low. "French-Canadian Folktales and Legends from Quebec and Acadia." In *Folktales Told around the World*. Edited by Richard M. Dorson. Chicago: University of Chicago Press, 1975, 429-67.

Lacourcière, Luc, and F. A. Savard. "Canadian Folk Tales Recorded during the Summer of 1948 in Charlevoix and Beauce Counties." Ottawa: National Museum, Bulletin 118, 1950, 63-65.

LaFollette, James E. *Étude linguistique de quatre contes folkloriques du Canada français*. Québec: Presses de l'université Laval, Archives de Folklore 9, 1969.

Laforte, Conrad. *Menteries drôles et merveilleuses. Contes traditionnels du Saguenay*. Montréal: Quinze, 1978.

Lambert, Adélard. *Contes de Tante Rose. Contes du Bon Vieux Temps pour enfants*. Montréal: Garand, 1927.

*Lanctôt, Gustave. "Contes populaires canadiens." *JAF*, 36(1923), 205-71; 39(1926), 372-449; 44(1931), 225-89.

——. "Fables, contes et formules." *JAF*, 29(1916), 141-51.

LaRue, Hubert. "Voyage autourde l'Île d'Orleans." *Soirées canadiennes*, 1(1861), 111-73.

Lemieux, Germain. *Contes populaires franco-ontariens*, I, II. Sudbury: Société historique du Nouvel-Ontario, 1953, 1958.

——. *De sumer au Canada francais*. Sudbury: Société historique du Nouvel-Ontario, 1968.

Les Jongleurs du billochet: conteurs et contes franco-ontariens. Sudbury: Société historique du Nouvel-Ontario, 1972.

——. *Les Vieux m'ont conte*. 10 t. Montréal: Bellarmin, 1973-1978.

——. *Placide-Eustache, sources et parallèles du conte-type 939*. Québec: Presses de l'université Laval, Archives de Folklore 10, 1970.

LeMoine, James MacPherson. *The Legends of the St. Lawrence*. Québec: Holiwell, 1898.

*Marie-Ursule, Soeur. *Civilization traditionnelle des Lavalois*. Québec: Presses de l'université Laval, Archives de Folklore 5-6, 1951, 184-268.

Massicotte, E.-Z. "Conte pour enfant. Les Bêtises de Jacquot." *Monde illustré*, 9(1893), 434-35.

——. "Feux-Follets." *Bulletin des Recherches historiques*, 35(1929), 645.

Massignon, Geneviève. "Les parlers français d'Acadie." *French Review*, 21(1947), 45-53.

Melançon, Claude. "Légendes de Percé." *Transactions of the Royal Society of Canada*, 16(1922), sec. 1, 113-20.

Michaud, Marguerite. "Un conte acadien. Conte de Bosquet." *L'Évangeline* (Moncton), 15 mars, 1948.

Montal, L. "L'Adieu de la Grise. Conte canadien." *Bulletin du Parler français*, 13(1915), 219-22.

Monteiro, George. "*Histoire de Montferrand: L'Athlète Canadien* and Joe Mufraw." *JAF*, 73(1960), 24-34.

*Morin, Victor. "Facéties et contes canadiens." *JAF*, 30(1917), 141-57.

Pare, A. "Légendes de l'Isle-aux-Grues." *Bulletin du Parler français*, 16(1918), 109-14.

Prud'homme, L.-A. "Quelques légendes du Nord-Ouest canadien." *Transactions of the Royal Society of Canada*, 18(1924), sec. 1, 131-48.

Rioux, Marcel. "Contes populaires canadiens." *JAF*, 63(1950), 199-230.

Rouleau, Charles-Edmond. *Légendes canadiennes*. Québec: Le Soleil, 1901.

Roy, Carmen. "Contes populaires canadiens." *JAF*, 63(1950), 199-260.

———. "Contes populaires de la Gaspésie." *Archives de Folklore*. 4(1950), 105-27.

———. *Contes populaires gaspésiens*. Montréal: Fides, 1952.

———. *Littérature orale en Gaspésie*. Ottawa: Musée national, Bulletin 134, 1955.

———. "La Petite Jument Bleue." *Amérique Française* (Montréal), 1949, I, pp. 56-73; "Les Sept Canardes," 1949, III, pp. 47-62; "Le Serpent au Teint Vert," 1950, III, pp. 61-77; "Le Magicien Balthazar," 1951, II, pp. 36-47.

———. *Saint Pierre et Miquelon: Une mission folklorique aux îles*. Ottawa: Musée national, Bulletin 182, 1962.

Roy, Pierre-Georges. "Légendes canadiennes." *Cahiers des Dix*, 2(1937) 45-92.

Schmitz, Nancy. *La Mensongère, conte-type 710*. Québec: Presses de l'université Laval, Archives de Folklore 14, 1972.

Skinner, Charles M. "Three Wishes: A Quaint Legend of the Canadian Habitants." *JAF*, 19(1906), 34-42.

Stevens, Paul. *Contes populaires*. Ottawa: G.-E. Desbarats, 1867.

———. "Le Père Mathurin." *L'Echo de France* (Montréal), 5(1867), 17-21.

*Tache, Joseph-Charles. *Forestiers et voyageurs*. 1884; rpt. Montréal: Fides, 1946.

Taschereau-Fortier, Marie C.A. *L'Ogre de Niagara*. Montreal: Levesque, 1933.

Tremblay, Jules. "Anecdotes de la Côte-nord, de Portneuf et de Wright." *JAF*, 33(1920), 259-72.

———. "La Vente de la poule noire: Anecdote canadien." *Transactions of the Royal Society of Canada*, 13(1919), sec. 1, 87-94.

*Tremblay, Malvina. "Contes de Chicoutimi et de la Malbaie." *JAF*, 32(1919), 101-12.

Turcot, Marie-Rose. "Trois contes populaires canadiens." *Archives de Folklore*, 1(1946), 153-72.

———. "Contes populaires canadiens." *Archives de Folklore*, 3(1948), 65-82.

Wallace, Paul A. W. *Baptiste Larocque: Legends of French Canada.* Toronto: Musson, 1923.

Warnock, Amelia B. (Katherine Hale). *Legendes du Saint-Laurent.* Montréal: CPR, 1925

——. *Legends of the St. Lawrence.* Montreal: CPR, 1926.

Wintemberg, W. J. "French-Canadian Folk Tales." *JAF*, 17(1904), 265-67.

Woodley, Edward C. *Legends of French Canada.* Toronto: Nelson, 1931.

Other References Cited

Aarne, Antti, and Stith Thompson. *The Types of the Folktale.* Helsinki: Academia Scientiarum Fennica, 1961.

Anselme (Chiasson), Père, and Daniel (Boudreau), Frère. *Chansons d'-Acadie.* Montréal, Pointe-aux-Trembles: La Reparation. II, 1945.

Barbeau, C. Marius. "Wyandot Tales Including Foreign Elements." *JAF*, 28(1915), 83-95.

Briggs, Katharine M. *A Dictionary of British Folk-Tales in the English Language.* 4 vols. London: Routledge & Kegan Paul, 1970.

Baughman, Ernest W. *Type and Motif Index of the Folktales of England and North America.* The Hague: Mouton, 1966.

Baum, Paul F. "The Three Dreams of 'Dream-Bread Story.'" *JAF*, 30(1917), 378-410.

Child, Francis James. *The English and Scottish Popular Ballads.* 5 vols. Boston: Houghton, Mifflin, 1882-1898.

Creighton, Helen. *Folklore of Lunenburg County, Nova Scotia.* Ottawa: National Museum, Bulletin 117, 1950; rpt. Toronto: McGraw-Hill, Ryerson, 1975.

Creighton, Helen, and Edward D. Ives. *Eight Folktales from Miramichi. Northeast Folklore,* 4(1962).

Fauset, Arthur Huff. *Folklore from Nova Scotia.* American Folklore Society, Memoir 24, 1931.

Fraser, Mary L. *Folklore of Nova Scotia.* Toronto: Catholic Truth Society, 1931; rpt. Antigonish: Formac, 1975.

Gagnon, Ernest. *Chansons populaires du Canada.* Québec: Bureau du Foyer Canadien, 1865, rpt. Montréal: Beauchemin, 1947.

Halpert, Herbert. "Tall Tales and Other Yarns from Calgary, Alberta." *California Folklore Quarterly,* 4(1945), 29-45; rpt. in *Folklore of Canada.* Ed. Edith Fowke. Toronto: McClelland & Stewart, 1976, 171-89.

Thompson, Harold W. *Body, Boots & Britches.* Philadelphia: Lippincott, 1939.

Thompson, Stith. *Motif-Index of World Literature.* 6 vols. Bloomington: Indiana University Press, 1966.

Waugh, F. W. "Canadian Folk-Lore from Ontario." *JAF*, 31(1918), 4-82.

Wintemberg, W. J. *Folklore of Waterloo County, Ontario.* Ottawa: National Museum, Bulletin 116, 1950.

Acknowledgements

Nos. 13 and 14, "The Cobbler" and "The Lousy-Head," are translations of "Le Pouilleux" and "L'Cordonnier," excerpts from *Civilization traditionnelle des Lavalois* by Soeur Marie Ursule, Les Archives de Folklore 5-6, Les Presses de l'Université Laval, Québec, 1951.

Nos. 4, 16, 17, 20, 24, 25, 26, 28, 33, and 34 originally appeared in *Folklore of Canada* by Edith Fowke, McClelland Stewart, 1976.

"Fearless Pierre," "The Carefree Miller," "The Winter of the Raven," "The Pumpkin Seller," and "Poucet and Marie" are translated from the *Journal of American Folklore* by permission of the American Folklore Society.

Printed by the workers of
Editions Marquis Ltée, Montmagny, Québec